FLAME
OF
POWER

Intimate profiles of Canada's greatest businessmen

OF

LONGMANS, GREEN & Co. TORONTO * NEW YORK * LONDON

FLAME

BY PETER C. NEWMAN

POWER

LONGMANS, GREEN & COMPANY
20 Cranfield Road, Toronto 16
55 Fifth Avenue, New York 3
6 & 7 Clifford Street, London, W.1

Copyright Canada, 1959
PETER C. NEWMAN

Jacket and book design by Gene Aliman   **Drawings by Lewis Parker**

I thought that my invincible power
would hold the world captive,
leaving me in a freedom
undisturbed.
Thus night and day I worked at the chain
with huge fires and cruel hard strokes.
When at last
the work was done,
I found that it held me in its grip.

SIR RABINDRANATH TAGORE

CONTENTS

FOR MY MOTHER AND FATHER

PROLOGUE

Power is for princes.

There is no man worthy of princehood in this book. Yet in each of the lives chronicled here exist elements of power far more telling than any contemplated in the brooding phantasies of the bravest of princes.

Man has always been alive to the itching in his palm. But only a few remarkable Canadians have evolved their acquisitive impulses into economic influence so immense that it grew beyond their control, like a forest fire that feeds on itself.

This is an examination in depth of the compulsive drive for business success that has been a major shaping force in Canadian history.

The businessmen in this book transformed Canada from a community of traders and land tillers into one of the world's economically most animated nations. They changed the history and the face of their country. They raised private armies and overthrew ministries. They stabbed the hump of mine headframes against the brumal blankness of the north. They erected the angular silhouette of factories across the urban twilight.

This is a short book about long lives.

It is a study of men, money, and the power wielded by their combination.

The mania of financial empire building dislodges satisfaction with common achievement. The men in this book were unable to transact business deals without becoming embroiled in them. In the process, they learned to rule their economic environment—to set themselves beyond the prosaic strivings and fallibilities of ordinary citizens. They constitute a tiny golden enclave in the context of Canadian development. Yet the least of them was possessed by economic audacity that erupted with astonishing consequences.

None of the men in this book inherited financial greatness. But their business fervour was such that during their lives they garnered personal fortunes aggregating more than a billion dollars. Their phenomenal mastery of the entrepreneurial art multiplied these funds a hundredfold, into policy control of over six hundred corporations with assets worth more than ninety billion dollars. They thus applied direction to capital a dozen times the value of all the Canadian currency that has been issued since Confederation.

The platoon of business tycoons chosen was not picked to encompass all the geographical or industrial expressions of

Canadian business power. The selection represents instead an attempt to personify the evolution of this country's economic thinking. It is a chronicling of fashions in high finance. The approach is biographical, but motives are analyzed as closely as results.

The book begins with the story of Sir Herbert Holt, an unremembered man without friends whose monomaniacal pursuit of money and power culminated in his becoming the richest Canadian who ever lived. During his reign there was scarcely a productive agency in the country that did not feel the pressure of his rivalry. Next is the account of the glacial Lord Strathcona, an aloof Labrador fur-trader who soared to a title and a business empire that included the country's three largest enterprises. A very different contemporary was Sir William Van Horne, a poker-playing extrovert who built the railway that united Canada, and then threw rails across two more countries.

With Sir James Dunn this history moves into another era. His princely habits were the gossip of an envious generation, but few recognized him as Canada's most daring industrialist. His hectic life ended more peacefully than that of Sir Harry Oakes, the gritty gold-seeker who accidentally found "the richest half mile in the world", and was hacked to death for his trouble. A contrast is provided by Lionel Forsyth, the studious one-time streetcar driver who became a romance languages professor, and then rose to head Canada's largest industrial complex.

Although he is not primarily a businessman, Gilbert LaBine, the wilderness-marked prospector who provided the uranium for the first atomic bomb, taught economic perseverance to less doughty colleagues. Told here for the first time is the story of the Steinbergs, five remarkable Montreal brothers whose artistry in merchandising has revolutionized the free world's shopping habits. Few men have had more amazing careers than Dr. Hans Lundberg, a Toronto geophysicist who has discovered minerals worth six billion dollars on four continents, and has actually grown gold. Canada's only economic dictator was Donald Gordon, head of the Wartime Prices and Trade Board—an unlovely, hot-tempered Scot who now rules the world's largest rail system. The book concludes with a study of E. P. Taylor, the much-hated but little-known promoter who has become the most spectacularly successful Canadian of his generation.

Taylor, Oakes, Holt, LaBine and Lundberg shattered traditional business concepts with new dimensions in economic exploitation. Dunn, the Steinbergs and Van Horne gained greatness by realizing in grandiose style the inspirations of less able predecessors. The contribution of Gordon, Forsyth and Strathcona was not so much to pioneer as to mesh group effort.

The men in this book share a common strain : they have been capitalists in the classic sense. They viewed the free enterprise system as a beneficial discipline, foreordained to reward the most able. They regarded the successful business corporation as the highest manifestation of man's superiority, and could recognize no contradiction in their belief that the larger a company can grow, the more perfect it becomes.

They listened with mounting bewilderment to the jeers of their detractors, but seldom bothered to reply. They could not understand why their actions required any justification under a system purporting the encouragement of individual enterprise.

They were rarely introspective, and even then could provide only vague, inarticulate hints about their motivation. Money was not a major prompting influence, only a measure of their achievement. But the power unavoidably lodged in wealth lost for them the perception to separate the deference awarded their riches from genuine personal respect. In some, the acquisitive momentum gradually developed into a convenient expression of inner disturbances. They came to regard themselves as contemporary inheritors of that mantle of esteem once carried by the gladiators, the noblemen and the bishops.

They consecrated a ritualistic energy to their work, denying themselves the release of total relaxation. Long past the point when added wealth or prestige could have any meaning, they continued to multiply their investments. Their labours were based on the catholic conviction that they could do certain things better than anyone else. They could not bear to discard such matters as legacy for those less competent.

While they may have succeeded brilliantly as individuals, they failed as a class. They could not adjust quickly enough to the new economic environment their own methods and way of living had helped to bring about. The business tycoon once was a social hero—proof to an invidiously competitive society that ability and application could be spectacularly repaid. But the mid-twentieth-century emphasis on man's fraternal interdependence has fostered the persuasion that the aristocrats of business do not, after all, represent the peak of human evolution. Money has come to be pursued more for what it will buy than for the power it can wield.

Business power in Canada has become reptile-quiet and discreetly housed.

Wealthy Canadians today live in large and comfortable homes, but nearly all the servant-infested mansions of their predecessors have either been shuttered, destroyed, or degraded to museum functions. Of the more than two hundred thousand men and women employed in domestic service three decades ago, fewer than eighty thousand remain. Canada's surviving three hundred millionaires have, with some exceptions, retreated into a self-imposed anonymity. The tycoon who formerly felt properly attired only with striped trousers, morning coat, cane and cigar, now indulges in studiously assumed informality.

The pomp that once flavoured big business in Canada is best preserved in a dozen exclusive clubs located discreetly in the main cities. Here, a man's privacy is still as sacred as his shaving-brush. The country's most impregnable businessmen's castle is the Saint James's Club, founded a hundred years ago by a group of Montreal merchants fed up with waiters eavesdropping on their noonday chatter. The only concession to the gaming instinct of its members is a rarely used billiard room. Much more popular are the *fauteuils* in the Club library which prop up a daily coterie of gently rumbling after-dinner dozers.

The most lasting contribution of the men in this book was their setting down of the foundations upon which has been erected the present structure of economic concentration in Canada. Through a mesh of intertwined directorships, about one hundred and twenty Canadians now possess a decisive measure of policy control over almost half the country's current material wealth, as expressed in factories, banks, railroads, mines, oil wells and other resources.

This financial aristocracy consists of an ever-altering list of names, with one group, then another surging forward while less adroit men are toppled. Membership in this economic *élite* is based on the holding of multiple directorships as a means of extending personal influence. By occupying the majority of the three thousand seats in the boardrooms of Canada's two hundred dominant corporations—as many as fifty directorships have been held by one man—this group has expanded the membrane of authority provided by a single company directorship into tiers and layers of grave economic consequence.

Company directors originate all business policies. They have the power to move factories without employees. They can hatch new towns by approving expansion blueprints, or, as one British Columbia court case proved, can sell the company's entire assets. They determine who will staff the top executive posts, and with how much authority. They allocate business profit between dividends and plowbacks. Because they hold the final responsibility for the corporation's well-being, they have become its operating owners. True, their might is perpetuated only through their election by shareholders. But the theoretically formidable power of the shareholders remains largely latent in Canada. Investors seldom take the trouble to attend annual meetings; they prefer to elect directors by mail on one-slate proxy forms sent out by the existing board, or, if they feel dissatisfied with directors' decisions, they sell their holdings.

A majority of Canada's currently powerful businessmen owe their fortunes to cumulative family transactions dating from pioneer railway, mining and industrial ventures— amassed wealth invested and re-invested with pyramiding benefits. The influence of this largely Montreal-centred group is gradually being eclipsed by Toronto, Prairie and B.C. financiers who believe that growth is more easily achieved by buying out one's competitors. Since 1900, three thousand major Canadian companies worth about five billion dollars have disappeared through mergers. Monetary marriages have reduced the number of Canadian banks from thirty-six to nine in the past fifty years. The United States, with roughly ten times Canada's population, has fifteen hundred times the number of banking institutions.

The effect of this corporate clustering has been to concentrate nearly half of Canada's industrial output in about two hundred corporations. That such a distillation of power has actually fostered rather than harmed Canadian development must be credited to the refusal by this country's businessmen to enter into any monolithic compact that might manipulate the national destiny to their advantage.

Canada's knights of business *do* constitute a small, self-perpetuating and enormously powerful *élite*. But it is a paradoxical kinship, maintained only through incessant jousting for position. This is no gentle prodding. It is battle waged with full Round Table vigour.

Not the fact of wealth but its use disrupts the common pattern of man's striving.

Only the rare individual possesses the inner balance to brandish great economic power without distorting himself in the process. It is with the remarkable manner in which this precarious balance of mind was struck by eleven of the most powerful businessmen in Canadian history that this book is concerned.

chapter 1

SIR HERBERT HOLT

He lived in the agony of self-imposed solitude.
He had no intimates and few diversions. He wove brilliant
and uncommonly intricate financial webs, remaining
always within a seldom punctured cocoon of anonymity.

THE remarkable economic power of Sir Herbert Holt
isolated him as a financial monarch even in an age when the
success of a man was judged by his millions, and the rich
inhaled the smoke of cigars wrapped in hundred-dollar bills
to savour properly the aroma of wealth. He was the only
businessman in Canadian history ever to match the influence
of a Rockefeller, a Carnegie, or a Ford.

Holt did not, as his enemies often charged, control the
fiscal policy of Canada. But he approached that stature closer
than any other Canadian before or since.

In the forty years before he died, on September 28, 1941, three hundred companies on four continents swelled under the tickle of his genius.

Holt's empire of ownership touched banks, mountains of ore, fur shops, hotels, streetcar systems, railroads, forests, flour mills, shipyards, theatres, life-insurance firms, and utilities in proportions so sovereign that were there a dozen men of his calibre, the Canadians of his time would have been left with little more than twelve outlets where they could sell their work. Canada in 1928 had paper money and coinage in circulation totalling $300 million. Holt in the same year was shepherding corporate assets worth nearly three billions.

Holt's financial accomplishments branded him so decisively as a money mogul that many Canadians, even in his lifetime, ignored his more practical achievements. He had been the engineer in charge of punching the Canadian Pacific Railway through the sliding-earth passes of the Rocky Mountains. In 1914 he designed the railroad transportation network which supplied the ammunition to halt the Kaiser's decisive thrust across France. During the sombre beginnings of World War II, he quietly gave Britain a full squadron of Spitfires.

When members of the 1934 House of Commons Committee on Banking and Commerce angrily insisted that Holt reveal the exact number of his corporate affiliations, he calmly replied: "I cannot tell you. I have never kept any record."

He was the president of twenty-seven major business enterprises and a director of about three hundred companies. They ranged from the giant Montreal Light, Heat & Power

Consolidated, which he founded, to a railroad through the Peruvian Andes that he had surveyed on mule back. Montrealers in the late 1920's complained : "We get up in the morning and switch on one of Holt's lights, cook breakfast on Holt's gas, smoke one of Holt's cigarettes, read the morning news printed on Holt's paper, ride to work on one of Holt's streetcars, sit in an office heated by Holt's coal, then at night go to a film in one of Holt's theatres."

In the days of multi-millionaire mystery men, Holt was the Canadian equivalent of Sir Basil Zaharoff, the secretive Greek who became the greatest armaments salesman in history, and Montagu Norman, the tradition-shattering Bank of England Governor. On the eve of the Depression, Holt was about to become the head of the world's largest corporation —Hydro-Electric Securities Limited, a utilities holding combine. He was well along with his plan to merge all Canada's primary steel producers into one giant monopoly under his direction. His mills were turning out 10 per cent of the world's newsprint.

During the twenty-six years of his presidency, he multiplied the Royal Bank of Canada's assets fifteenfold. Before it was expropriated by the Quebec government for $112 million in 1944, his Montreal Light, Heat & Power Consolidated became the largest privately owned utility in the world. Holt seldom saw a movie; but Famous Players Corporation, which he organized, introduced Canadians to the talkies, and still dominates the industry.

Holt's economic legacy includes the commercial seigniories out of which have grown such key Canadian firms as the Consolidated Paper Corporation, the Dominion Textile

Company, Canada Cement, and the Dominion Steel & Coal Corporation.

The mention of Holt's name could impart stock market fortunes their breath, or garrotte them without appeal. When shareholders of Brazilian Traction, Light & Power panicked during the 1925 revolution in Sao Paulo, rumours were leaked to the floor of the Montreal Stock Exchange that Holt was becoming a company director. The sell-off stopped although the revolution continued and Holt never did join Brazilian's board.

Holt was not a business administrator. He promoted his fortune by refining the sleight-of-hand process involved in the acquisition of corporate control through the trading and re-trading of stock. His was a legal legerdemain of unmatched proportions.

Holt's spectacular instinct for potentially profitable business situations gained him international stature. "Sir Herbert is the business brain of Canada," wrote London's *Daily Express* in a 1926 editorial. "He holds a position in the commercial and industrial life of the Dominion, for which it is impossible to find any parallel. He is certainly a more important figure in the Canadian world than the Prime Minister is in that of Great Britain."

To his less successful commercial rivals, to the leaders of the burgeoning union movement, and to left-of-the-middle politicians, Holt was a symbol of the obsolescent business aristocracy which could so easily be blamed for the country's economic difficulties. Holt believed devoutly that business was a dog-eat-dog proposition; and he did not propose to be eaten.

He fought publicity as a hot gospeller fights the devil.

When he subscribed to charity, and this was not often, it was on the condition that the source of the funds would not be revealed. Montreal wags of the day claimed that when some of Holt's blood was used in a transfusion for one of his grandchildren, the youngster froze to death.

During the 1931 strike of the Canadian Union of Linemen & Helpers against his power companies, Holt's life was threatened so often that Montreal papers all had his obituary set and waiting in their composing rooms. But Holt refused to give up his morning habit of walking to work. He marched through downtown Montreal, enclosed in a square formed by four guards with cocked rifles. A year earlier he had ducked under his mahogany desk barely in time to avoid the bullets of a deranged stockbroker.

Holt had none of the bankerish characteristics associated with his type.

Three inches over six feet, he walked with the heavy gait of a tugboat skipper, flexing his knees to compensate for the roll of an imagined ship. His face resembled nothing so much as a carefully washed and smoothly polished Irish potato punctured by pinched, garter-blue eyes. The broad, crew-cut head bulged as if straining to hold in the turmoil of its contents. His rain-grey suits and stiff white collars, with their encircling funereal neckties, fitted him with the awkwardness of a staunch Presbyterian minister's go-to-picnic outfit. He had an irrational hatred of barbers.

Holt lived in the agony of self-imposed solitude. He had no intimates and few diversions. He wove brilliant and uncommonly intricate financial webs, remaining always within a seldom punctured cocoon of anonymity.

"Sir Herbert," according to R. O. Sweezey, a Montreal

investor who often fought with him, "was a ruthless, lonesome old cuss with no friends, but fundamentally sound and honest."

Holt wanted it said of him that he had been a power. "He was quite determined to get on in the world," remembers his son, Herbert P. Holt, a retired British Army officer. "Probably his two chief characteristics were a passion for efficiency and a love of work for its own sake."

Holt's closest associate was Sévère Godin, who was his private secretary for thirty-seven years and later became one of French Canada's richest business men. "Sir Herbert," Godin recalls, "wanted everyone to think that he was a man of steel. Actually, he was lonely and extremely shy."

At odd moments Holt's solicitude melted the passionless brutality of his business manner. During the seesaw negotiations which eventually resulted in the formation of the huge Canada Power & Paper Corporation, he took time out to show the young Rowan Coleman (later Director of Placement at McGill University) how properly to knot a necktie.

Holt's private life was prudishly spartan. Pleasures were entered into reluctantly, rather than being used to counterpoint the frets of the office. "Most tired businessmen," he would tell his luncheon companions at the Mount Royal Club, "get tired because of the things they do *after* business hours."

He tried golf, but stomped off the green arguing about the number of strokes he had taken. He slept an invariable seven hours, never drank, seldom smoked. After dinner, he often went for a walk along the south side of Sherbrooke Street. Alone and unrecognized, he watched the games at the Westmount Lawn Bowling Club.

Montreal society's gossip highlight of 1931 was an account
—more highly coloured at each telling—of the first time
Holt played bridge in the Mount Royal Club. At the end
of a lost rubber, Holt socked his dull partner in the jaw.
The game continued without explanation or apology. But
next day a club member appeared carrying a shotgun, ex-
plaining that he feared he might be asked to play with Sir
Herbert.

The incident was not uncharacteristic of Holt's temperament. Once in Chicago he rushed to the defence of a woman
being held up by two armed men. He slugged one of the
bandits so hard that he was nearly booked on a manslaughter
charge. During the building of the C.P.R., he flattened two
drunk section hands, fumblingly trying to murder him, by
cracking their heads together.

When he was seventy-six he took a mineral-bath cure at
Karlsbad, in Czechoslovakia. In two days he became bored
with the chatter of old men. He climbed a nearby mountain,
slipped near the summit and tumbled down a cliff, partly
paralyzing his right side. Two years later he suddenly joined
the Montreal Light Aeroplane Club.

He did not buy an aircraft, nor did he ever own a yacht.
He had no holiday home until 1935. Then he built a small,
frescoed mansion on Hog Island in the Bahamas, where he
spent most of his last five winters.

Holt's three-storey stone house on Stanley Street in Montreal impressed its visitors as being more of a mosque than a
rich man's comfortable sanctuary. The large entrance hall
was backed by a floor-to-ceiling fireplace with set-in family
crests. A drab dining-room led into the main drawing-room.
Though always spotless, it conveyed the musty mood of a

first-class railway carriage. Fourteen bedrooms and seven bathrooms were spread through the top two floors.

Lady Holt, the quietly dignified daughter of a Sherbrooke industrialist, filled many cupboards with her china collection, later willed to the Montreal Museum of Fine Arts. Among the home's distinguished but never advertised guests was the Duke of Windsor, who stayed briefly with Holt during his 1927 Canadian tour. Sir Herbert did not give up his master bedroom for the royal visitor. The house was demolished in 1942 to make way for office construction.

Just after eight every weekday morning, Holt walked the mile and a half from his house, past the Craig Street pawnshops, to his third-floor office in the Montreal Power building. He was chauffeured to directors' meetings in a 1912 Rolls-Royce. Because the automobile operated satisfactorily, Holt kept it six years. He was shocked when two young C.P.R. clerks bought the Rolls for commuting to work.

Holt's office manners were those of a compulsive housewife. He worked behind a desk as big as a dining-room table in a puritanically unadorned, forty-foot-long room. Objections from subordinates were cut off with stiff finality. "You," he would say, "have had a bad brainstorm." Holt spent most of each day dictating letters to his chief assistant, Sévère Godin, at a staccato pace of two hundred words a minute. Godin seldom talked about Holt outside the office. When he did, it was usually to assure the legion of doubters that in his opinion, "Sir Herbert is the greatest Canadian that ever existed."

Holt accepted invitations to business luncheons on the condition that he would not be asked to speak. According to his son, he detested publicity in any form : "There are no family records bearing on his career. My father was born in an age when life was taken seriously and he retained this outlook up to the time of his death."

Holt's contemporaries could understand him no better than the historians. He did not live according to the mores of the society in which his wealth placed him. It was a time when rich Montrealers looked to the late Victorian and Edwardian days for inspiration. A man was judged by how he disposed of his cherry pits.

Probably the most idle of Canada's idle rich at that time was Elwood Hosmer, the son of Charles Rudolph Hosmer, president of Ogilvie Flour Mills. Elwood spent most of his days drinking gin and smoking cigars in one of the lobby lounge chairs at the Ritz-Carlton Hotel, often answering nature's calls in the pot of a nearby palm tree. His manner of living was climaxed daily at six P.M., when Elwood—his chair surrounded by the accumulated droppings of his day's smoking—would pass out, half covered by the funny papers which were his favourite reading. Bellboys would then carry him outside where a chauffeur would transfer him to his limousine for the two-block drive home. This routine was seriously disrupted only once. Elwood suddenly decided he wanted to fly the Atlantic. The attempt ended with his aircraft crashing a few minutes after take-off, and he soon was back in the more stable Ritz-Carlton arm-chair.

It was also an age of a conspicuous consumption in which Holt did not wish to share. Sir Henry Pellat, who made most of his fortune bringing hydro power from Niagara Falls, built himself Casa Loma in Toronto. It has ninety-eight rooms, fifteen marble-floored bathrooms, twenty-three fireplaces and a kitchen oven big enough to roast simultaneously three oxen. Melba McMartin, the daughter of the prospector who helped grubstake the discovery of the Hollinger gold mine, bought a sixty-four-carat diamond the size of a man's thumb joint, but only wore its paste imitation. Her cousin Jack used to march into Montreal bars and with his walking stick smash every bottle behind the counter. Weary bartenders let him enjoy himself, because they knew they could charge him a flat $1,000 fee per performance. Despite such antics, the McMartin fortune proved to be amazingly durable. When Melba's brother Duncan was an R.C.A.F. instructor near Calgary during World War II, one Friday the pay packet failed to arrive and he wrote out a cheque to cover the station's payroll.

Holt could easily have outdone any of the country's richest spenders. Instead, he furiously continued to build up his fortune without demonstrating to the world either its extent or his personal feelings. Although he headed the Royal Bank of Canada for nearly three decades, and his portrait adorned the bank's $5, $10, $20 and $100 bills, his files in the bank's morgue contain only the copies of his speeches to annual meetings.

The only personal data Holt ever passed for publication was the antiseptic description of himself in the Canadian Who's Who as "Civil Engineer and Capitalist." In 1938 Frederick Griffin of the Toronto Star wrote Holt for an appointment, promising a favourable story. "I am," Holt replied, "certain that anything favourable you might write about me would only give the Communistic yellow press another opportunity to vilify and lie about me; consequently, I think it better to continue my past policy of not appearing in the press." Concluded the Star in an editorial, "Sir Herbert is quite nice to newspaper reporters, as long as they don't come near him. He does not believe in charity and has little faith in hope."

When one well-known Montreal writer was commissioned to prepare a profile of the financier, he was received in Holt's office and told : "As long as you print nothing libelous, I suppose I cannot prevent you. But at least I won't aid or abet you." The project was dropped.

One of the few newspapermen permitted to spend an afternoon with Holt was the financial editor of *The Times* of London, who visited Montreal in 1914. "I had seen the archbishop, who wanted to pick me out a French-Canadian wife, and Van Horne, who kept me five hours talking about painting and philosophy," he wrote. "But this man Holt seemed to inhabit a world absolutely foreign. He sat behind a desk at the end of a long office, so that everybody coming to talk to him was inspected *en route*. He spoke like a high priest, and convinced me I should never like to be his private secretary."

Holt's few public predictions were frosted with an almost divine pessimism. J. H. Gundy, the Toronto financier who was one of his closest associates, once told a friend, "If I had to eat lunch with Sir Herbert every day, I would be the greatest pessimist in Canada." In 1934, Holt predicted another crash and warned all his company officers to sell their stocks. He continually advocated amalgamation of the C.N.R. and C.P.R. as the only alternative to national bankruptcy. But there was wisdom also in his doom-calling. "People do not realize the Russian menace," he said in 1931. "The spread of Communism is not a matter to laugh at."

Holt was a lukewarm Anglican. His politics were Conservative "But," a colleague remarked, "Sir Herbert really understood nothing about politics except how to manage Cabinet ministers." During the Depression Holt had a brief and involuntary brush with political power. Marcel Desbois, leader of the Montreal Association of French-Canadian Youth, urged the province's young men to overthrow the government. Desbois calculated his coup would save two million dollars in annual administrative charges. He named Holt as the "General Manager of Quebec" at a salary of $250,000. Holt sent the job offer to the police.

A less bizarre but much more useful public-service request came from the British Government soon after the outbreak of World War I. The War Office asked Holt to apply his railroading experience in planning the war-zone French railways. For two months he stalked around the trenches studying the army's *matériel* requirements. Then he outlined an emergency transportation system. It was mainly responsible for providing the Allies with enough ammunition to halt the Kaiser's initial attacks. The 1915 honours list of George V rewarded him with a knighthood.

When he returned to Canada, the *Montreal Gazette's* marine editor asked Holt about conditions in England. "You may think," said Holt, "our politics bad enough, but the politics of the mother country are absolutely rotten. We will never win the war until a strong man is found in England to direct the business end of the war." The ensuing uproar greatly strengthened Holt's resolve never to allow reporters beyond his reception chamber.

Holt was an enemy of paternalism in any form. He believed that Canada offers every man the opportunity for financial independence and that charity is bad because it keeps people from working. He continually frustrated those who approached him as a symbol of the philanthropic millionaires of his age. His gift to the machine-gun battery organized by Sir Clifford Sifton in 1914, for instance, consisted of a little cash and the recommendation of a young recruit, who, wrote Holt, "owns a first-class motorcycle which he is willing to place at the service of the Empire."

But he could be generous. In 1910 he financed the Typhoid Emergency Hospital in Montreal. When Dr. E. A. Garrow, a Montreal surgeon, successfully operated on him, Holt overpaid his modest bill, took over the management of the doctor's investments and made him a millionaire. His largest donation was a cheque for $250,000 to Canada's Wings for Britain fund in 1941. In a thirty-two-word note, he asked that the money be used to buy a squadron of Spitfires.

Holt had little time or patience for community projects. In 1916, however, he became chairman of the Federal Plan Commission set up to redesign Ottawa and Hull into a properly impressive capital. His 160-page report suggested the rearrangement of Ottawa's railway lines much as it was later completed by the National Capital Commission. He also recommended a dramatic alternative. This would have eliminated level crossings by burying the railroads in an east-west crosstown tunnel. Holt's report predicted a 1950 Ottawa population of 250,000—within fifteen thousand of the actual count.

That Holt was able to find such a gainful asylum in the mazy orbits of high finance was due in part to his tough business indoctrination in Canada's early railway construction camps. He landed in this country during the 1875 depression —a freckled nineteen-year-old civil engineer, freshly graduated from Trinity College in Dublin, his birthplace. His first job, surveying the Toronto islands for waterworks installations, brought him in contact with James Ross, later one of the C.P.R.'s builders and an early Canadian coal baron.

Ross hired Holt to be assistant engineer for the laying of a crude lumbering line called the Victoria Railway, running from Lindsay, Ontario, north into the Haliburton bush. Two years later, Ross picked him as his superintendent of construction for the Credit Valley Railway, now part of the C.P.R.'s main Montreal–Windsor line. The road's credit was at first so poor that part of Holt's job was to collect the fares at Parkdale, the Toronto terminus, take the money to a nearby dealer, and buy enough coal for each trip.

While he was building the Credit Valley, Holt awarded his tie contracts to William Mackenzie, a schoolteacher turned lumberman, later co-builder of the Canadian Northern Railway with Donald Mann. Holt at this time was living with his brother and sister in a Toronto boarding-house, and saving twenty-five dollars out of his thirty-five-dollar pay each month.

When in 1883 Ross was awarded the major contract for C.P.R. construction west of Winnipeg, he took Holt with him as his chief engineer. A year later Holt resigned to form his own construction firm. His first contract was for grading near the mouth of the Kicking Horse River. On a surveying expedition from the head of the Kicking Horse Pass to the Columbia River, his horse shied and knocked him down a cliff. He somersaulted on top of a dead tree caught in the canyon's wall, almost thirty feet below the trail, and was pulled up, just in time, with a lariat secured across his chest.

When Holt's construction gangs reached the Selkirk

Range, the C.P.R. temporarily ran out of funds. The gambling bosses at nearby Beavermouth, deprived of their income, fanned the men into a strike mood. Holt armed his clerks with all his available weapons—nine Winchesters and six revolvers—threw a log across the trail from Beavermouth and waited with six-shooter drawn. The army of strikers, many of them carrying rifles, marched toward Holt's platoon. "The first man that crosses that log, I shoot," Holt warned them. "We have guns enough to take care of the hundred and fifty of you. Now you know." Not a man moved.

In the last eighteen years of the nineteenth century, Holt became one of Canada's most active railway builders. With Mackenzie, Ross and Mann, he threw 550 miles of track across the Prairies (from Macleod to Edmonton and from Regina to Prince Albert); he built most of the C.P.R. links through the Rockies and the Selkirks; he helped design and was in charge of constructing many of the pioneer lines in New Brunswick, eastern Quebec and Maine. A railroad stop near the summit of Kicking Horse Pass where for a time he made his headquarters, now known as Lake Louise Station, was originally called Holt City.

Provision was made for Holt to be in the front row during the driving of the last C.P.R. spike at Craigellachie, B.C., on November 7, 1885. But when he was asked where he stood during the ceremony, he said : "I wasn't there, I was too busy." He couldn't attend because he was repairing the still shifting rails west of Revelstoke to ensure the safe passage of the inaugural train.

Mackenzie and Mann, both later knighted, went on to build the ill-fated Canadian Northern. Ross undertook the rehabilitation of Toronto's horse-car transportation system.

Holt permanently deserted the contractor's car in 1901 and moved to Montreal.

The city was at that time served by eighteen small gas and electricity firms distributing energy with lottery-like efficiency. Holt became the largest shareholder in the Montreal Gas Company, founded by leading citizens in 1848, and merged it with the Royal Electric Company to form Montreal Light, Heat & Power Consolidated.

During the next twenty-three years, he methodically swapped stock in his company for the shares of his competitors, crushing those who wouldn't sell. By 1924 he had a monopoly of the energy distribution on Montreal Island and controlled the city's tramways system.

Herb Holt, the railroad builder, had become Sir Herbert Holt, the financier. Stockbrokers marvelled at his intuitive market touch. Each share in Montreal Light, Heat & Power Consolidated, originally worth $100, had by 1925 multiplied in value to $1,140. Royal Electric stockholders who had paid $15 dollars for their shares in 1896 owned, by 1925, M.L.H. & P. Consolidated stock worth $185.

Most Canadian corporate quarrels are settled in a broadloomed hush, between the walnut panelling of boardrooms. Holt provided a dramatic exception by challenging Sir Adam Beck, the founder and chairman of the Ontario Hydro-Electric Power Commission, to a strange public duel. Beck had told a reporter that Holt's stock manipulations had forced the price of Montreal electricity from $42 to $75 per horsepower. Holt exploded. He offered $10,000 to any charity named by Beck if he could prove his charges. "The challenge isn't worth the time required to pick it up," Beck replied.

In 1924 Lord Atholstan, the founder and publisher of

the *Montreal Star,* ran a series of well-documented articles revealing the details of how Holt had dangerously watered the Montreal Light, Heat & Power stock structure. Values of the shares tumbled thirty-nine points.

Frantic investors clamoured for Holt to make a statement. He refused to defend his company. Instead, he quietly ordered his brokers to buy up the depreciated stock. As values gradually recovered, Holt's calculated silence netted him more than a million dollars' profit.

Holt extended his power empire to the international level in 1926 by joining the board of SIDRO, a Belgian holding trust with effective control over fifty utilities including the huge Mexican Light & Power and Barcelona Traction, Light & Power. The president of SIDRO was Captain Alfred Loewenstein, one of the world's least known, yet most influential businessmen.

In 1928 Loewenstein wanted to amalgamate his holdings with Holt's properties into a trust called Hydro-Electric Securities Limited. In terms of its controlled assets, it would have been the world's biggest corporation. Holt agreed, with one provision : that he would become the merger's president.

To settle the preliminaries, Holt sent Godin to Loewenstein's New York hotel room. The talks started badly. The European financier travelled with a staff of forty and wanted at least a dozen assistants to witness the negotiations. Holt's man insisted on privacy. Godin finally sketched out the anatomy of the world's largest company while squatting on the ledge of Loewenstein's bathtub. The wet, cornered Belgian agreed to Holt's presidency while soaping his armpits.

The ambitious arrangement ended abruptly on July 28, 1928, when Loewenstein leaped into the English Channel during a private flight from London to Brussels. His secretaries testified at the inquest that he had opened an exit instead of the washroom door by mistake. But many were of the opinion that it had been suicide; air pressure would have made the difference in doors obvious. Others believed that he had never been on the plane, but had entered a Catholic monastery in England. The London press reported he had run off with a Yugoslav beauty.

Holt eventully became the dominating influence in sixty-five power companies, including the municipal systems of Monterrey in northern Mexico, Baltimore, Calgary, Fort William, Sydney, N.S., the Okanagan Valley and most of Quebec. In 1919 he financed the Andean National Corporation which snaked a 350-mile pipeline across the Republic of Colombia for the Tropical Oil Company.

An earlier diversification was his purchase of the Colonial Bleaching & Printing Company, a small Montreal textile mill, in 1903. Two years later Holt engineered a merger with Dominion Cotton Mills and some smaller firms into the Dominion Textile Company. He and three other investors put $100,000 each into the charter syndicate, then captured control of the other firms through share-exchange offers. (In the process, Holt got back $1.66 for every dollar he had invested in Colonial Bleaching.) Dominion eventually became Canada's largest textile manufacturer. The company paid dividends of fifteen million dollars on its original underwriting.

Holt defended his profits from the deal before a 1936 Royal Commission investigating Dominion Textile's closing of its Sherbrooke mills in protest against the competition of imports.

"What," demanded Commission Counsel J. C. McRuer, "is your justification of attempting through the protection of tariffs to earn 150 per cent yearly on your investment?"

"It is the result of thirty-one years of good management," replied Holt, "and if you consider the original risk, I think it quite right that sufficient remuneration should be earned."

"So your view," McRuer snapped back, "is that you can put as much water into a stock as you like, and earn dividends on it."

"It was *not* water," Holt insisted.

The lawyer barked back: "I'll call it water, you can call it what you like."

Holt became a banker in 1902, when he was named president of the Sovereign Bank of Canada. This was a small, specialized institution; its main asset was the financing of the Alaska Northern Railway being built to bring out Alaska's coal. Holt tried unsuccessfully to alter this lack of diversification. In 1905 he called Sévère Godin into his office and dictated his resignation. "I feel that I cannot continue responsibility without authority," he wrote. Three years later, when the U.S. banned the export of Alaska coal, the Sovereign was declared insolvent.

Holt had meanwhile become president of the Royal Bank of Canada, which then had 100 branches and assets of about $50 millions. He captained the Royal for twenty-six years. In that time, assets increased to $750 millions, and the number of branches jumped to 688.

Holt brought his instinct for merger to the Royal's presidency. He bought out the Union Bank of Halifax, the Colonial Bank of London's branches in the West Indies, the Traders Bank, the Quebec Bank, and the Northern Crown

Bank. "Holt did more to build this bank than anyone else," said Sydney Dobson, for a time the Royal's president under Holt's chairmanship. "He had a strong character and because of his stature was able to influence business to the bank." Just before Holt died, the Royal outgrew the Bank of Montreal, fulfilling one of his great ambitions. It has since become the world's seventh largest bank.

Holt's banking connection cost him the presidency of the Canadian Pacific Railway. He had been a C.P.R. director and member of the executive committee since 1911. He was nominated for president in 1918, but that would have meant a switch of the railroad's banking account to the Royal from the Bank of Montreal, and the latter had enough representatives on the board to kill the appointment.

Not all of Holt's interests were in huge corporations. He was one of the syndicate of rich Montrealers who invested two million dollars in 1913 to build the Ritz-Carlton Hotel, intended as a refined roost for important visitors. He also was the key promoter of Famous Players Corporation, organized in 1920 to establish the first major chain of Canadian moving picture theatres. In 1929, just after talkies were introduced, the 153 Famous Players theatres drew thirty-two million Canadians. The country's population was then just over ten million.

Holt's most ambitious scheme, launched when he had passed seventy, was his attempt to weld all of Canada's steel producers into a super-corporation with assets of more than a billion dollars. As a start, he paid $50 million for control of the British Empire Steel Corporation in Sydney. He added to it an assortment of thirty associated industries, renamed it the Dominion Steel & Coal Corporation, and made it into what was then the biggest industrial empire in the country. Holt remained a Dosco director until 1941, but his plans for further mergers were thwarted by his inability to interest the Steel Company of Canada and Sir James Dunn's Algoma Steel.

Holt attempted a similar agglomeration of the pulp and paper industry with his 1929 formation of the Canada Power & Paper Corporation. It was conceived as an extension of the St. Maurice Paper Company—a 1925 Holt merger of three Quebec paper firms. St. Maurice acquired the Belgo-Canadian Paper Company to become the St. Maurice Valley Corporation. The Laurentide Company was then brought in, its shareholders being given one share and a hundred-dollar debenture in Canada Power & Paper Corporation for their stock.

The Thunder Bay Paper Company, Wayagamack Pulp and Paper, Port Alfred Pulp & Paper, and Anglo-Canadian were similarly absorbed, so that by 1929 Canada Power & Paper had assets of $250 millions, timber limits half the size of the British Isles, and mills turning out one-tenth of the world's newsprint.

The acquisitions had cost Holt little cash. To snare each corporation he merely ladled out more Canada Power & Paper stock. He had enough representational strength on most of the recruited companies that the acceptance of his offer was little more than a formality.

To provide his mills with more pulpwood, Holt bought the Island of Anticosti, a virgin, whale-shaped stand of fifteen million cords of timber at the mouth of the St. Lawrence River.

Anticosti had been discovered by Jacques Cartier in 1535. Henri Menier, a French chocolate manufacturer, bought it for $125,000 in 1895, built a *château* at Port Menier and stocked his retreat with salmon, beaver, deer, caribou, and moose. Holt's Anticosti Corporation bought the island for $6.5 millions, not including fishing rights on the Jupiter River, a famous salmon stream. Holt sent in three thousand lumberjacks and built five ships to bring the wood to his mills.

Because of the high initial investment, Anticosti timber cost ten dollars more per cord than any other Canadian pulpwood. The shareholders of Anticosti bitterly referred to their company as the "Ain't-It-Costly Corporation." In 1934 they realized three dollars on an average original per-share price of ninety-four dollars.

As the Depression of the thirties cut world demand for newsprint, the shares of Canada Power & Paper plummeted from a 1929 high of ten dollars to a 1931 low of one dollar. The capacity of Canadian paper mills had doubled between 1925 and 1930; exports to the U.S., the principal market, had nudged up only 20 per cent.

All the companies in the industry suffered, but Canada Power & Paper was hit hardest. Its timber limits, because of their location, could not be economically co-ordinated with its scattering of mills; a fantastically inbred management insisted on the priority of inter-company obligations; and the dead weight of the extensive carrying charges and its bloated capitalization nearly tumbled the company into bankruptcy. Shareholders rioted at annual meetings, demanding withdrawal of their original companies from the floundering dinosaur.

Into this hysterical financial jamboree, Holt injected salvation with desperate grandeur. Canada Power & Paper would, he promised, absorb Abitibi Power & Paper, the St. Lawrence Corporation and the Backus-Brooks Canadian interests, making it a $500 million enterprise controlling the production of a quarter of the world's newsprint. The move would have left only two major Canadian pulp and paper companies outside Holt's grasp.

But it was too late. No new recruits were willing to become part of Holt's elephantine venture. His vision of a pulp and paper empire was snuffed out on October 31, 1931, when the Canada Power & Paper Corporation was replaced by the Consolidated Paper Corporation. Shareholders received one Consolidated share for ten in the old company. Consolidated eventually became Canada's third largest paper maker, but it didn't recover from its debt-ridden birth sufficiently to pay dividends until March 1946.

The 1929 crash destroyed any notion of Holt's immunity to financial flops, but left his personal fortune only slightly dinted. His position was at no time in jeopardy. According to Sydney Dobson, the former Royal Bank president: "Sir Herbert got out of the market in time. He never played on margin."

"Whatever may have been the result of the crash," recalls his son, "I noted no change in my family's way of living."

Holt's personal funds provided a life-buoy of solvency for many associates during the Depression. One company he didn't help was a well-known but badly over-extended Montreal investment firm. When one of the firm's partners was told that Sir Herbert had instructed the Royal Bank to carry his company no longer, he tried to shoot Holt. His bullets missed. But the man, thinking that he had committed murder, went home, locked his garage doors, started his car and sat behind the steering-wheel until he suffocated.

Holt's death at eighty-five, on September 28, 1941, came from the shock of having stepped into an overheated bath. "More than anyone else," wrote London's *Daily Express*, "Sir Herbert made Canada great in peace and powerful to defend her greatness in war." The *Montreal Gazette* summed up his career: "Not only was he the richest man in Canada, but his activities, direct and indirect, covered a field which for variety was unequalled by those of any financier in the world."

Eight carloads of flowers followed Holt's coffin out of St. George's Anglican Church. But even in death he presented Montreal society with a dilemma. Senator Lorne Webster, another of Canada's great business princes, had died five hours before Holt and was being buried an hour later at Dominion Douglas United Church. Most of the mourners thought it more diplomatic to be seen at Webster's funeral.

Holt's name survives in none of his corporate creations. Holt, Renfrew & Company, which he controlled, was not, as many contemporaries believed, named after him. The firm's title commemorates a Quebec City fur-trader called John H. Holt, who died in 1915.

Holt received his public elegy on the day of his death. During the International League baseball game at Montreal's Delorimier Stadium, the bottom of the fifth inning was interrupted by the rude blat of a loudspeaker announcing: "Sir Herbert Holt is dead."

The crowd hushed, whispered. Then cheered.

chapter 2

L O R D   S T R A T H C O N A

His empire-scale manipulations touched the lives
of many men, leaving them with a brooding sense of disquiet,
like the first of a month of rainy days.

Most Canadians think of Lord Strathcona only as a bearded
history-book gentleman in a swallow-tailed coat, uncomfortably bashing in the last spike of the Canadian Pacific Railway. Behind this fuzzy public memory is the most remarkable
business career in Canadian history.

Strathcona was probably the last of his type.

His empire-scale financial manipulations touched the lives
of many men, leaving them with a brooding sense of disquiet,
like the first of a month of rainy days. Although he spent
more than half his manhood in tattered exile as an obscure

Labrador fur-trader, Strathcona more than any other business man became a major determining force in the early evolution of Canadian economics and politics.

His astounding skill as an international financier made possible the construction of the C.P.R.—a feat that united the country economically as Confederation had politically. During his four decades as Governor of the Hudson's Bay Company, he transformed a dominion of wilderness into a commercial enterprise. As its President for twenty-seven years, he made the Bank of Montreal Canada's largest financial institution of the time.

Strathcona is rarely remembered now as a statesman but his diplomacy settled the first Riel rebellion and his dramatic political turnabout toppled Sir John A. Macdonald's first Canadian government. Even less well remembered is the fact that Strathcona was responsible for the establishment of the predecessors to the Royal Canadian Mounted Police and Canada's reserve army.

When Lord Strathcona died at ninety-four, in 1914, he had outlived most of the violent animosities that he created as plain Donald Alexander Smith. During the last three decades of his life—alone left of his generation—he listened to his legend and began to believe it.

He wished desperately to be remembered not only as a man who had never sinned, but as a man intrinsically incapable of sinning. He regarded his House of Commons seat as a patriotic trust, and would not accept his M.P.'s salary. Yet he was tossed out of Parliament for bribing voters to re-elect him, and the success of his companies depended on the loans and stock options his agents distributed to ministers of both parties.

His contemporaries were sharply divided in their verdicts of Donald Smith and his achievements.

Sir John A. Macdonald bluntly declared : "That fellow Smith is the biggest liar I ever met." W. T. R. Preston, the chief Ontario Liberal organizer, wrote : "The Smith syndicate was entirely responsible for using Canadian Parliament for the most improper purposes that ever became operative among a free people."

Those who defended Smith were equally vocal. After presenting him with the tenth of his twelve honorary degrees, the Very Reverend Daniel M. Gordon, Vice-Chancellor of Queen's University, proclaimed ; "As a Canadian, I am grateful to God for the large service He has enabled Lord Strathcona to render for Canada."

Because Smith spent the first thirty years of his business life forgotten in Labrador, the record of his appearance is almost entirely that of his old age. He liked to picture himself as a Viking prince, moving the limbs of his six-foot frame with military precision. The formidable penthouse of his gnarled brows gave his snow-squinted eyes a telescopic effect. When he spoke there was not a quiver in his meticulously trimmed beard. His sentences were ridiculously cumbersome, lacking any flash of wit.

Rather than use a word of abuse, even in the most aggravating circumstances, Smith preferred merely to signify his agreement with the oaths of an underling. On the night of his humiliating defeat by Manitoba voters in 1880, for instance, he remarked to James Cole, a Hudson's Bay factor : "I am sorry to say that a majority of the intelligent electorate of my late Selkirk constituency have, in the exercise of their undoubted privilege and right to choose the most fit and proper person available for the purpose of representing them in the Dominion Parliament, seen fit to reject my own humble, not hitherto unacceptable person."

Cole described the upset more succinctly : "The damn voters took your money and voted against you !"

"You have properly expressed the situation," Smith replied.

During the decades before and after the turn of the century, Smith was one of Canada's best-known, if not best-loved, public figures. Invitations to the many receptions at the largest of his four homes—a baronial red-stone castle at 1157 Dorchester Street—were sought by every social climber in Montreal. Smith was a snob to the point of keeping a secret guest tally, classifying his visitors according to rank. The impressive roll call included a future king and queen (George V and Queen Mary who came to Canada in 1901 as the Duke and Duchess of Cornwall and York), a prince and princess, eight dukes, seven marquises, twenty-one earls, six viscounts, six governors-general, twenty-six lieutenants-governor, seven prime ministers, twenty-seven provincial premiers, four archbishops, seventeen bishops, twenty-nine supreme court judges, fourteen chief justices, thirty-one mayors and fifty-eight generals. (Smith's list even separated this last group into forty-seven generals of the Imperial Army and eleven colonial troop commanders.)

The dining-room of the house opened into a garden for summer teas often attended by more than two thousand guests. When the future King and Queen of England stayed with Smith, he built a special balcony off the second floor so that the royal couple might have a better view of the fireworks display exploded from the top of Mount Royal in their honour.

The home's custom-made furniture was carved out of bird's-eye maple; bisecting the house was a dramatic three-storey staircase, all its mahogany components faultlessly dove-tailed with wooden pegs. Below stairs and out of hearing a row of eight rooms was partitioned off for the more than a dozen maids and flunkeys.

Fitted more by temperament than by birth for the aristocratic life, Smith ruled his household with humourless mastery. Once while he was eating breakfast with Dr. Wilfred Grenfell, he watched the lamp under the hot water kettle falter and die. When the missionary wanted to relight it, Smith stopped him and angrily summoned his butler. "Remember, James," he said, "you have only certain duties to perform. This is one. Never, under any circumstances, let such an omission occur again."

Such arrogance was particularly maddening to those who remembered Smith's inconspicuous background. He was born on August 6, 1820, at Forres, a Scottish milling town in the middle of that brooding countryside where Shakespeare pictured Macbeth and Banquo meeting the doom-happy witches. His adolescence was much less influenced by his father—a tradesman clinging to solvency with alcoholic indecision—than by his uncle, John Stuart. Stuart had been second-in-command during Simon Fraser's exploration of the Fraser River's headwaters in 1808, and later became factor of the Hudson's Bay Company trading post on Lesser Slave Lake. Following his unspectacular graduation from the local grammar school, young Donald began to toil as a clerk in the office of the town lawyer.

When he was eighteen, John Stuart came home on furlough and offered to recommend him for a junior clerkship in the Hudson's Bay Company. The youngster accepted eagerly. In May, 1838, a year after Queen Victoria had succeeded her uncle on the British throne, he sailed for Canada aboard the *Royal William,* a five-hundred-ton timber-trade windjammer. Much of Smith's fifty-day voyage was spent reading about the country of his destination. The main reference in the ship's library was Evans' *Guide to Canada.* Mr. Evans' advice was more well-meaning than informative. "Canada is a country," he wrote, "where immigrants should not expect to eat the bread of idleness, but where they may expect what is more worthy to be denominated as happiness—the comfortable fruits of industry."

Smith landed in Canada at a time when nationalist stirrings were reaching their culmination in the Mackenzie and Papineau rebellions. British North America then had a population of 1.2 million. The country west of Ontario belonged to "The Governor and Gentlemen Adventurers of England Trading into Hudsons Bay" under a charter granted by Charles II in 1670, as an inducement to find a north-west passage—a task the company never took seriously. Inside the quarter continent they ruled, Hudson's Bay officials made all the laws and enforced them. They could marry a man, or hang him; they coined money, raised armies and fought wars. At its peak, the company's power extended into Russia, Alaska, California and Hawaii.

Montreal, at the time of Smith's arrival, was a puppy bush settlement with a population of barely thirty thousand; its only patch of sidewalk was the approach to Notre Dame

Cathedral. McGill University consisted of a medical faculty with two part-time professors.

Smith's first job was counting muskrat skins in the stuffy Hudson's Bay warehouse at Lachine, for "twenty pounds a year and all found." For three years he lugged around the stacks of pungent pelts. Then he was promoted to junior trader at Tadoussac, an isolated St. Lawrence River trading post near the mouth of the Saguenay. There he spent the most unhappy and unproductive years of his life.

Being forced to mature away from a world he had just begun to know, but where he felt the things in which he wanted to participate were happening, he began to feel the gnawing need for self-assertion which never left him. The pressures which made him one of the most frigid aristocrats of his era had their roots here, on his lonely treks through the Saguenay forests, apparently forgotten by his world.

When his cabin caught fire during the summer of 1847, Smith fed the flames with his clothes and private papers, cackling incoherently in hope-exhausted frustration. That fall he began to feel the symptoms of increasing snow-blindness. His requests for compassionate leave were repeatedly denied.

When the schooner *Marten* called in at Tadoussac on her way to Montreal, he deserted. After Montreal doctors had examined him and declared there was nothing wrong with his eyes, Sir George Simpson, the autocratic Hudson's Bay governor, punished Smith for breaking the rules by assigning him to the company's version of hell : North West River (now Fort Chimo), a derelict trading post in the north-east corner of Labrador.

The North West River station was tucked into a clearing

on the shore of Hamilton Inlet, a hundred-mile-deep salt water gash in the frowning eminence of the unexplored Labrador coast. With mountain ranges rolling out of both horizons in the mammoth undulations of a tornado-whipped ocean, the little outpost appeared to be an unwanted chunk of flotsam at the edge of the world.

During his thirty years in Labrador, Smith acquired the insensibility to both hatred and loyalty which later allowed him twice to betray his political allegiances and to promote some of the most questionable deals in Canadian business history. Yet the local Indians and Eskimos regarded him as such a benevolent monarch that after he became rich, a delegation of Nascopies journeyed all the way to Montreal and demanded that Smith buy Labrador, kick out the Moravian missionaries who followed him, and become its king.

"It wasn't solitude for me," Smith reminisced about Labrador. "I knew everybody there from the oldest white trader to the youngest Indian hunter and his dogs. I was always busy, and when I had no definite task, I was planning." Smith was the third white man to follow the Hamilton River up from its mouth at Goose Bay to the awesome view of Grand Fall—a wilderness-encased waterfall twice the height of Niagara, where the river plunges over a 302-foot precipice into Bowdoin Canyon with a roar audible fifty miles away.

Dressed in a flaming flannel shirt and homespun trousers, Smith spent most of his time bartering blankets and tobacco for furs. He also acted as judge and doctor. His treatment of wounds with a pulp made from the boiled inner bark of juniper trees was later studied by Lord Lister, who introduced the principles of antiseptics to surgery in 1865.

To provide himself with a city diet, Smith sent to the

Orkney Islands for poultry, to Quebec City for a dozen cattle, six sheep, some goats and an ox. On seven painfully cleared acres, he grew turnips, cucumbers, potatoes and peas. To connect his farm with the trading post, he built a two-mile track for his ox-drawn sulky—Labrador's first road. With the remarkable foresight that characterized his later decisions, Smith demanded that the Hudson's Bay Company assign a trained geologist to North West River. "I believe," he wrote Governor Simpson, "that there are minerals here which will one day astonish the world." His superiors ridiculed the requests and refused to act on them, even after he had sent them samples of "magnetic iron". Diamond drills have since confirmed that Smith's "area of astonishing minerals" contains commercial quantities of iron ore, titanium, lead, zinc, nickel, asbestos and colombium, as well as a dyke of uranium eighty-five miles long that may prove to be the world's largest radioactive ore body.

As the fur revenues of North West River declined, Smith began to trade in seal oil and established a lively export business with Britain in Labrador cranberries and salmon packed in ice. He even built a small but not very successful cannery. After Sir Leopold McClintock, the British Arctic explorer, surveyed the Labrador coast for the best landing-place of the trans-Atlantic telegraph cable, he reported on Smith's unusual activities to the Hudson's Bay Company board of directors in London. "Labrador won't hold that man much longer," he predicted.

Smith had meanwhile married Isabella Hardisty, the daughter of a retired army officer. She had come north with her family and had married James Grant, one of Smith's fellow traders, but without church ritual. A few months later she changed her mind and picked Smith as her husband. The marriage was legalized half a century later in a secret ceremony at the British Embassy in Paris.

Smith returned to England for a holiday in 1864 and so impressed Hudson's Bay officials in London that five years later he was transferred out of Labrador to Montreal as the company's chief factor. Canada was then barely two years old. Electricity was still considered a risky innovation, the telephone and typewriter had not yet appeared. Talk at the Saint James's Club concerned the purple imagery in the latest rhymes of Alfred, Lord Tennyson, and William Gladstone's surprising eloquence in the British House of Commons.

The bearded Labrador trader came to the company's Canadian headquarters at a strategic moment. The new Federal Government had just completed negotiations in London for the purchase of nineteen-twentieths of the Hudson's Bay territories for $1.5 million. The transfer might have been uneventful but for the *métis*—six thousand French half-breeds who farmed around Fort Garry in southern Manitoba. They resented the company's disregard for their rights through settlement and feared the domination of a centralized, English-speaking Protestant government. The incendiary spark was provided by Louis Riel, a fanatic partially educated for the priesthood, called by Smith "a remarkable but ill-balanced man." Riel and his followers marshalled the discontent of the Fort Garry settlers, urging either annexation to the United States or formation of a separate republic.

It is doubtful whether many Canadians today realize by how delicate a margin the Prairies were saved for Canada. "The tendency of North American events is plainly towards the consolidation into one great nation," chirped the *New*

York Sun in 1871. "From the Polar Sea to the Isthmus of Darien, there will in time be only one national government—that of the United States. Who among us can say that ours is not a glorious destiny or reflect without exultation that he is an American citizen?"

The Canadian Government sent surveyors to the Prairies with instructions to parcel the land into mile-square sections, with no regard for the traditional strip-farming methods of the French and half-breed settlers. The move rallied Riel's supporters. They stopped William McDougall, the Ottawa-appointed Governor of the region, from entering his territory at Pembina (now Emerson, Manitoba) and captured Fort Garry.

In Ottawa, Sir John A. Macdonald realized that the country did not have adequate transportation facilities for the dispatch in winter of troops to quell the rebellion by force. Because Hudson's Bay Company interests were so vitally concerned, he appointed Smith Government Commissioner to investigate the insurrection. After a two-week journey by train, stagecoach and sleigh, Smith reached Fort Garry on December 27, 1869. Riel promptly arrested him. At a public meeting in the Fort Square three weeks later, he allowed Smith to proclaim Ottawa's intentions. Icicles hung from Smith's beard as, standing beside Riel in a numbing twenty-below wind, he promised fair treatment to the mustered settlers. The meeting elected forty representatives to study the proposals. In an attempt to reassert his authority, Riel executed Thomas Scott, a particularly quarrelsome Portage la Prairie Orangeman.

When Smith returned to Ottawa, he recommended that an armed expedition be sent to Fort Garry in the summer to reimpose the rule of law. The troops entered the Fort on August 21, 1870, without firing a shot. In his report to Macdonald, Smith also suggested that a permanent semi-military force should be established in the region. This resulted in the formation of the North West Mounted Police, predecessors of the Royal Canadian Mounted Police.

Smith capitalized on his popularity with the Fort Garry settlers by winning the Winnipeg seat in the first Manitoba legislature. He became federal M.P. for Selkirk in 1871. But politics occupied little of his time. He was quietly becoming one of the new Dominion's up-and-coming tycoons.

Named the Hudson's Bay resident governor in 1871, he realized the potential of the assets retained by the company after the sale of the greater part of its lands to the Crown. He foresaw that where buffalo grazed, cattle would one day feed, and that much of the prairie was favoured with two hours more sunshine a day during the wheat maturing season than any other farming region in the world. While other shareholders panicked, he bought up great blocks of Hudson's Bay stock at depressed prices. He gradually acquired enough shares to exercise a working control of the company. On some of this stock he later realized a 1,300 per cent profit. He changed the emphasis of the company's operations from fur to land. So much of its remaining territory was sold by Smith that the Hudson's Bay Company eventually had to repurchase chunks of it for the construction of department stores at many times the original price.

Smith's business reputation prompted many of the Hudson's Bay factors to send him their savings for investment. With these funds and his own growing fortune, he captured stock control of the Bank of Montreal in 1887. For the next twenty-seven years he was the Bank's president, backing many of Canada's most profitable early commercial enterprises. He personally bought a textile mill at Cornwall and built a railroad rolling-stock plant in Montreal.

The flagrant business piracy which accompanies the embryonic stage of most developing economies dominated Canadian railroad construction in the last quarter of the nineteenth century. The twenty-six thousand miles of railway line operating at the beginning of World War I were built with government cash subventions and bond guarantees totalling $489 million. Ottawa also gave the railroad promoters more than fifty-six million acres of land, and some of Canada's best timber and mineral tracts. Yet every mile of railway track in the country was privately owned. During the heyday of railway building, one C.P.R. lobbyist boasted that whenever the Speaker's bell rang for a division, there were almost always more M.P.'s in his apartment, drinking free liquor and puffing free cigars, than anywhere else in Ottawa.

Building of the C.P.R. was the dominant issue in Canada's fledgeling Parliament for thirty years, especially after British Columbia made a railway link with the East a condition of Confederation. Smith became a central figure in the first attempt to finance a trans-continental railway.

Sir Hugh Allan, head of Montreal Steamships and sixteen other important telegraph, coal, iron, cotton, tobacco and paper companies, was promised a Government grant of fifty million acres and $30 million for the syndicate he organized to build the line. To enlist the support of Donald Smith— by then Macdonald's most influential back-bencher—Allan included him on his provisional board of directors, and proposed giving him $100,000 worth of stock.

The scheme exploded in Parliament on April 2, 1873, when the tabling of confidential correspondence revealed that Sir John A. Macdonald had given the charter to Allan in return for $350,000 in election fund contributions. A royal commission confirmed the bribery attempt, forcing Macdonald's resignation. Had he been able to gain parliamentary support, however, he could have picked his successor, possibly even retained his Party in power.

When the vote which would determine the fate of Canada's first Parliament was approaching, Smith was in the West. Macdonald ordered him back. "Upon you," he wrote, "and the influence you can bring to bear, may depend the fate of this administration." When he arrived in Ottawa, Macdonald tried to get a pledge of support from him, but Smith would say only that he would support his party if he might do so conscientiously.

The night of the crucial debate, November 5, 1873, was a cloudless, moon-washed autumn evening. The galleries were packed; visitors overflowed onto the floor of the House. At five minutes after one, Smith rose. "I would be most willing to vote confidence in the Government," he said, as the treasury benches yelled support, "if I could do so conscientiously." Then speaking in the hushed tones of a judge pronouncing his verdict, he dealt the death blow: "For the honour of the country, no government should exist which has a shadow of suspicion resting on it; and for that reason, I cannot give it my support." (The more cynical commentators of the time were convinced that what *really* bothered Smith was that the Government's contract with Allan did not give him personal control over the C.P.R. charter.)

Smith's speech nearly caused a riot in the House. Macdonald, incoherent with rage, shouted at him, "Coward! Mean, treacherous coward!" Later he remarked to one of his Cabinet ministers, "I could lick that man Smith quicker than hell could frizzle a feather." Those who sat in the galleries that evening claimed that only the presence of the Sergeant-at-Arms and the immediate dissolution of the House prevented fisticuffs between Macdonald and his former supporter.

In the election that followed, Smith returned to the House as one of the most influential members in the Liberal Government under Alexander Mackenzie, a working stonemason who had led the Opposition during Macdonald's régime. Smith fought hard for his seat under his new colours. "His audiences," reported a writer of the times, "were abundantly supplied with eggs of an uncertain age." He won by 102 ballots, but his even narrower margin in the next general election was ruled illegal. To guarantee victory, he had temporarily transferred twenty-six Hudson's Bay families into his riding, and bribed them to vote for him. A Manitoba judge, Mr. Justice Betourney, confirmed Smith in his seat, but when a reporter discovered that Smith held a four thousand dollar mortgage on the judge's home, a Supreme Court appeal reversed the decision.

Smith's parliamentary expulsion was humiliating; but he had long before switched most of the spare-time interests that his Hudson's Bay governorship allowed him to railroading— then the country's most profitable industry. With his cousin, George Stephen, he formed a syndicate to buy the defunct

St. Paul & Pacific Railway from its Dutch bondholders. The road had been started in 1857 as a link between Minnesota and the west coast, but the Civil War intervened after the completion of only 217 miles. Construction had originally been financed through the sale of $28 million worth of bonds to Dutch investors. By the time Smith became involved, interest on the securities had not been paid for seventeen years; the unhappy Dutchmen sold their holdings for less than a quarter of their par value. Smith renamed his property The St. Paul, Minneapolis & Manitoba Railroad (now part of the Great Northern), extended its tracks into Winnipeg, and quickly made it one of the continent's most profitable railroads.

This venture convinced Smith that he should somehow obtain a major financial interest in the building and operation of the C.P.R. Although he was probably the only member of the Mackenzie Government who fully appreciated the problems of railway building, he allowed the Liberals to flounder with the project as a federal enterprise. During the five years of the Mackenzie regime, only a hundred miles of track were laid. Partly because of the Government's obvious incompetence in railway building, Macdonald was returned to power in 1878. Two years later, persuaded that the C.P.R. would be built faster by private interests, Macdonald awarded the charter to George Stephen, then the Bank of Montreal president and a major shareholder with Donald Smith in the St. Paul, Minneapolis & Manitoba Railroad.

The terms were so generous that W. T. R. Preston, the Ontario Liberal organizer, called the deal "the most stupendous contract ever made under responsible government in the history of the world." The railway company's loans, cash subsidy and capital stock guarantees eventually amounted to $206 million. Completed government roadbeds were transferred to the C.P.R. without charge. The land grant consisted of twenty-five million acres given in alternate sections of 640 acres in a belt twenty-four miles deep on each side of the tracks, with deficiencies in fertile lands made up in other regions. The C.P.R. was also promised a twenty-year railway monopoly in its western areas, perpetual tax exemption over part of its lands and extraordinary authority over passenger and freight rates. In return, Stephen's syndicate guaranteed to complete the work by 1891.

Although Smith and Smith's money provided a major support of the C.P.R. syndicate, his name was left off all company papers and government submissions, in case Macdonald, remembering his treachery, would grant the charter to one of the other interested groups. Smith organized the Canada North West Land Company to get the maximum profit from the territorial land grants. Nearly five million of the free acres were eventually sold to settlers at an average price of six dollars per acre. Smith and other members of the C.P.R. syndicate sold themselves treasury stock at twenty-five cents on the dollar, ensuring personal profits even before the first locomotive was purchased. Smith officially became a C.P.R. director in 1883. For the next decade he was the most influential member of the board's executive committee.

The ruggedness of the terrain which William Van Horne, the construction chief hired by Smith and Stephen, had to cross rapidly drained the company's treasury. Stock sales went badly. Dutch bankers, disillusioned by their loss on the St. Paul & Pacific and other railroads, campaigned in European money centres to discredit the C.P.R. securities. Many of the shares had to be sold for ridiculously low prices. Canadian banks floated loans up to their limit. Smith, Stephen and the other directors threw most of their personal fortunes into an ever more hopeless race with construction payrolls and supply bills. Finally, only a further appeal to the Government for more cash could save the venture. Van Horne sent Smith a coded cable in the spring of 1884, which climaxed the hunt for funds : "Have no means paying wages, pay car can't be sent out. Unless you send immediate relief, we must stop."

In one of his rare short sentences, Smith summed up the C.P.R.'s plight. "It's to the government, or to the penitentiary," he told Stephen. When Macdonald was first approached about giving the C.P.R. more funds out of the federal treasury, he flatly refused. "You may as well ask," he declared, "for the planet Jupiter as for more money." But the C.P.R. directors decided to remain in Ottawa. "The day the C.P.R. busts," one of them remarked, "the Conservative Party busts the day after."

During a Party caucus which followed the interview with Macdonald, Tory members agreed to vote an extra subsidy, provided some way could be found of humiliating Smith for his treachery of 1873. Smith was told that the C.P.R. would get the money only if he agreed to contest a Montreal constituency in the next election, not just as a Tory, but as a personal admirer of Sir John A. Macdonald. Smith agreed. He re-entered the House as the Conservative member for Montreal West but rarely attended sittings.

Riel's second rebellion provided the transport business that finally saved the C.P.R. The railroad was completed on November 7, 1885. The first trans-continental consisted of Smith's private car, *The Matapedia,* Van Horne's *Saskatche-*

wan, an engine and a baggage car. Smith climbed off the train at Craigellachie, a flag stop in Eagle Pass in the Monashee Mountains, to pound the last spike through its iron holding plate into the wooden tie. His first blow merely turned the head of the spike over. Roadmaster F. B. Brothers yanked it out and replaced it with a new one, which Smith carefully tapped in with slow, measured strokes. (The engine that pulled the historic train was scrapped, *The Matapedia* burned to her trucks at Princeton, B.C., in 1925, but Van Horne's private car has been preserved by the Canadian Railroad Historical Association. The maul used by Smith to pound in the last spike was last seen in the basement of his Montreal house, being used to break coal for the furnace. The spike itself was cut into pieces which were set with diamonds to make brooches for the wives of the financiers mainly responsible for the C.P.R.'s construction.)

A year after the railroad's completion, Smith was knighted. He remained member for Montreal West until 1896. Afraid that he might swing behind the new Liberal leader, Sir Wilfrid Laurier, the Tories appointed the seventy-six-year-old financier-politician Canadian High Commissioner to the United Kingdom.

London society immediately adopted the former Labrador fur-trader as its favourite colonial character. Queen Victoria called him "His Labrador Lordship", or, in kinder moods, "Uncle Donald." "You talk with him," wrote A. G. Gardiner, editor of the *London Daily News,* "and it is as if Canada stands before you, telling her astonishing story."

The *Montreal Star* campaigned for the naming of Smith as Governor-General of Canada, but he put down the suggestion, preferring his life in London. When the Queen elevated him to the peerage in 1897, he chose as his official crest a beaver gnawing a maple tree. As "Baron Strathcona and Mount Royal, of Glencoe, in the County of Argyll, and of Mount Royal, in the Province of Quebec and Dominion of Canada", he represented this country in London for eighteen years. His appointment, oddly enough, was extended both by Laurier and Sir Robert Borden, his Conservative successor.

He worked twelve hours a day. The lights of his office on Victoria Street burned late so often that the building was nicknamed "the lighthouse." During one holiday in rural England, he began dictating letters to a newly hired secretary on Sunday morning. The assistant politely but firmly declared that he could not work on the Sabbath. Smith paced his room all day, and promptly at midnight woke up his startled clerk with the command : "The Sabbath is now over. We must make haste with those letters !"

Under his direction, the first Canadian immigration offices were opened in London. The trans-Atlantic flow of Englishmen increased from 10,000 in 1897 to 138,000 in 1912. On one immigrant-hunting trip to Hamburg, he was so successful that the German Government officially notified Canada it would arrest Lord Strathcona if he ever returned to entice away the country's productive citizens.

In the last two decades of his life, Smith's business interests were limited to the stock market and his governorship of the Hudson's Bay Company. The C.P.R. shares he had acquired for $25 reached $280 within his lifetime. This investment, plus his profitable holdings in the Hudson's Bay Company, the Bank of Montreal and other enterprises including the Dominion Steel Corporation, the Anglo-Persian Oil Company and the Laurentide Company, made him one of the richest Canadians of his day. Finally in a position to compensate for the hardships of his decades in Labrador, Smith became the country's most generous philanthropist.

He gave away $12 million during his lifetime; $20 million in his will. Easily his most dramatic gift—and probably the most deliberately spectacular action in his life—was his donation in 1900 of a fully equipped mounted regiment to help the British fight the South African War. Smith analyzed reports of the Boer successes against the sedulously drilled British infantry and quickly recognized the need for a mobile troop of mounted scouts. He offered a million dollars to raise the Lord Strathcona's Horse—an army of six hundred North West Mounted Police veterans. Volunteers included a hundred adventurous Arizona cowboys who offered to enlist their own horses, but Smith turned them down.

In the fall of 1900, the troops travelled by train across the country to their embarkation headquarters at Halifax. Well-wishers thronged them at every stop. The citizens of Sudbury presented Colonel S. B. Steele, the commanding officer, with a battle flag on which was stitched the earnest tribute : "We are proud of the Empire. We are proud of our Queen. We are proud of Lord Strathcona." The regiment fought in South Africa for a year with considerable success.

After its much-heralded return to England, Strathcona entertained his army at a banquet in London's Savoy Hotel. "The occasion of his own toast being drunk," *The Times* dutifully reported, "produced the wildest enthusiasm, the officers and men springing to their feet, making the roof echo with their ardent cheering." During World War I, the Strathconas were part of the Canadian Cavalry Brigade. In World War II, they fought with distinction in Italy and northwestern Europe as part of the 5th Armoured Division. A, B and C squadrons were sent into action again in 1950 as front-line replacements in Korea.

The gift of the Strathconas gave Smith a world-wide reputation for philanthropy. All the requests for financial aid in his mail were placed on a silver tray. Every Sunday he would fish out a dozen or so. Those which satisfied his strict tenets of being "properly deserving" received a donation. Sometimes he would write for more details. One exception to this ritual occurred during his time as Canadian High Commissioner in London. A youthfully arrogant tramp ordered Smith's secretary to inform him that he was the son of the man who had driven young Donald to Aberdeen when he had left home to sail for Canada. The tramp came out of Smith's office with a five-pound note. Next day he was back. He received more money. But when he was announced again, Smith quietly told his secretary : "Give the gentleman another five pounds and tell him he need not return. You may add that his father did not drive me to Aberdeen. I walked."

Smith's biggest gifts were to English, Canadian and American universities and Montreal hospitals. He financed the university education of nine young Montreal girls in 1884. Nicknamed "the Donaldas", they were the first women admitted to McGill. He donated a million dollars to found Montreal's Royal Victoria Hospital and gave the Grenfell Mission two hospital ships.

In his will, Smith divided $6 million among McGill, Yale, Cambridge and the University of Aberdeen. He also set up the half-million-dollar Strathcona Trust for Physical and Patriotic Education in Canada—the forerunner of Canada's reserve army. It still operates from Ottawa, allocating about thirty thousand dollars a year for school cadet equipment, scholarships for physical training instructors, and other activities "designed to foster a spirit of patriotism in young boys, leading them to realize that the first duty of a free citizen is to be prepared to defend his country." The strangest section in his will provided for the cancellation of debts owed him by the estates of Sir Richard Cartwright and Sir George Foster—finance ministers in the Liberal and Tory governments during the C.P.R. negotiations. While there was no evidence of bribery, the personal necessities of these men that made them borrow from Smith may have influenced their governmental decisions.

Despite his liberal philanthropy, Smith never forgave Manibota voters for his defeat at the polls in 1880. He donated no charitable dollars to Winnipeg schools or hospitals during his lifetime, and mentioned none of its institutions in his will. He timed his return from an inspection of the railroad's Rockies section in 1909 so that he would pass through Winnipeg at midnight. A deputation of citizens waited to greet him. There was no invitation to enter his darkened private coach. His secretary insisted that he could not possibly allow His Lordship to be disturbed.

Although he understood little about painting, Smith during his last years brought together one of North America's finest private art collections. He had works by Raphael, Titian, Gainsborough, Reynolds, Romney and Constable. Most of the canvases were donated to the Montreal Museum of Fine Arts by his descendants in 1927, when his house was sold to Lord Atholstan, the *Montreal Star* publisher. (The latter converted it into a home for elderly Presbyterian ladies of good but bankrupt Montreal families. The building was destroyed in 1941 to make way for an office skyscraper.)

Smith made the error of many successful men in holding onto his power after age had diminished his capacity for rational command. In the last years he became unbearably stuffy. When he heard that W. H. Duff-Millar, the Agent-General for New Brunswick, had ordered a ceremonial uniform for a royal reception, he tracked down the tailor. Work on the outfit was stopped when Smith personally visited the shop and furiously insisted that as far as he was concerned, provincial agents-general had no official standing, and were therefore not entitled to special dress.

Lord Strathcona died of a heart attack at five minutes to two, on January 21, 1914. His snobbery extended beyond the grave. His will directed that money be set aside for the establishment of a leper colony. But it had a strict entrance requirement—only leprous English gentlemen of good standing could be admitted.

chapter 3

SIR WILLIAM VAN HORNE

*To each day he gave his talents
with such vigour
that he made all the ingredients of his rich life flourish,
while he increased the world's and his own material assets.
He could recognize no contradiction in his belief
that one had to make money to give life its full expression.*

WILLIAM CORNELIUS VAN HORNE was born in 1843 at Chelsea, in Wills County, Illinois, the son of an impoverished lawyer. He died at Montreal in 1915, a British knight and a multi-millionaire, mourned by the land he had welded into a nation through his building of the Canadian Pacific Railway—a task of dimensions greater than any on this continent could ever be again.

During his eleven years as president of the C.P.R., Van Horne transformed a debt-saddled pioneer line into the world's largest transportation system. He became dominant in thirty major Canadian corporations, then gave up his C.P.R. career to fling railroads across Cuba and Guatemala.

In an age of specialization, Van Horne multiplied himself in an incredible diversity of directions. He was an untrained but academically honoured botanist and palaeontologist; a dozen of his best paintings are now hung at the Montreal Museum of Fine Arts. He was the inventor of a grasshopper killer, an avalanche deflector, and a submarine finder, and even plotted the St. Lawrence Seaway half a century before it was built. "I would operate it twelve months of the year, and have it bordered with electric lights that would turn night into day," he recommended.

Van Horne was many times a millionaire and one of the most powerful men of his generation, but money and power were to him only the desirable complements to the enormous zest he expended in his frantic drive for achievement.

To each day he gave his talents with such vigour that he made all the ingredients of his rich life flourish while he increased the world's and his own material assets. He could recognize no contradiction in his belief that one had to make money to give life its full expression.

As plump as a bearded Bacchus, Van Horne could propel his chubby limbs with remarkable agility. His frequent chuckling swelled inevitably into blasts of belly-pumping laughter. His bull-like head, the forehead high and bald, sloped sharply down into the disproportionately large, hairy nose. A gourmand on the prodigious scale, he informed Moberly Bell, managing director of *The Times* of London, after he had been dubbed a knight by Queen Victoria, that the Van Horne coat of arms would be "a dinner horn pendent upon a kitchen door." He accompanied his nightly poker games by munching biscuits heaped with black caviar, washing them down with neat whisky. During his railway inspection tours, he would telegraph ahead to the next stop for two roast-chicken dinners, then eat them both.

At the office Van Horne blew cigar smoke into the faces of his callers with the punctuated impudence of a spouting whale. During his last sickness his doctors strictly limited him to three cigars a day. Van Horne meekly agreed. But by next morning he had a box of specially rolled two-foot perfectos brought to his deathbed, and so puffed contentedly the prescribed three a day, for four hours each.

Van Horne died on September 11, 1915, three weeks after an unsuccessful abdominal operation. The entire C.P.R. system was halted in silent homage for five minutes. Cuba declared a day of national mourning. "He did more for us in one year," said Mario Menocal, the Republic's president, "than Spain did in four centuries."

His body was taken for burial to Joliet, Illinois, his ancestral home, by the *Saskatchewan*, the private coach in which he had so often travelled over his railroad. He loved to climb aboard at the very moment his train was scheduled to start, and would roar at the conductor if it was a minute early or late. The car was constructed entirely of mahogany, its interior panelling glowing dark red in the light of the brass lamps. The master compartment had a brass bedstead riveted to the floor.

Few men have nourished such flamboyant ambitions and even fewer have lived to witness their fulfilment. Yet Van Horne believed that he had not properly utilized even a fraction of his capacity. "When I think of all I could do," he said as he lay dying, "I should like to live five hundred years." One of the projects he had planned but never begun was his autobiography. "I've just been too damn busy to cast a thought so far back as my grandfather," he complained.

He was a descendant of Jan Cornelissen Van Horne, follower of Peter Minuit, the parsimonious Dutch West India Company trader who in 1626 purchased Manhattan Island from the Iroquois for trinkets worth twenty-five dollars. His father abandoned a prosperous New York law practice to farm at Chelsea, an Illinois log-hut village near the departure point of the old Oregon Trail. When William, the first of five children, was eight, the family moved to Joliet, near Chicago. The senior Van Horne revived his legal practice, but he died suddenly in the 1854 cholera epidemic, leaving a good name, much debt and some bad accounts receivable.

Young William's schooling lasted exactly six years. He was expelled at fourteen after he was caught drawing caricatures of his teachers—an art he practised at home by disfiguring sketches of American authors in *Harper's Magazine*. The disfigurations of the rather stuffy gentlemen were so good that his mother protested to her friends about the editor's shocking bad taste in treating famous writers so disparagingly.

Van Horne first helped to support his family by making a copy on a large sheet of wallpaper of the Crystal Palace—the huge London pavilion built for the Great Exhibition of 1851. Little Willie then nailed the painting to castoff blind rollers, and while two boy assistants swung the contraption from side to side, he collected a penny each from the customers who came to watch the panoramic effect thus produced.

The youngster's Sunday hobby was to burrow into cliffs around Joliet, searching for fossils. His palaeontological hunt became so absorbing that when he saw a perfect trilobite outline embedded in a stone slab on the town's main street, he returned at night with a hammer and chipped it out. During a lifetime of Sunday fossil gathering, Van Horne discovered and classified many new specimens. Nine have officially been called after him, bearing the descriptive suffix : *van hornei.* His collection was willed to the University of Chicago.

This geological interest was the initial directing influence of Van Horne's career. He was so fascinated by Hitchcock's *Elements of Geology,* lent him by Augustus Howk, a school chum, that he copied the volume's 262 pages in longhand into five nickel scribblers—illustrations, footnotes, bibliography and index. "Transcribing that book did great things for me," he said later. "It showed me how much can be accomplished by application." He tacked his newly discovered ambition to a definite goal : he would become a railroad superintendent so that he might ride to work in a private train.

After the abrupt ending of his formal education, Van Horne spent most of his time at the local Illinois Central Railroad station, studying the tap of the telegraph instrument when he wasn't delivering telegrams. He became a fully qualified telegrapher on his fifteenth birthday.

Van Horne retained a Morse key for practice in his C.P.R. presidential car thirty years later. Once at his company's New York telegraph office he heard a communication coming in for him. "Here is your message, Sir William," said the clerk. "Yes, and here is my answer," Van Horne immediately replied. He had received the dots and dashes with one hand, while writing his reply with the other.

His slack routine as a telegrapher at Joliet gave Van Horne a chance to understudy most of the stationary jobs in railroading. He exercised his memory by reciting the car numbers of passing freights. His first invention was a primitive cold storage to help preserve the butter shipments of local farmers.

His career as a telegrapher was ended suddenly a year later. He had wired a steel plate in sight of his office to give passing yardmen a mild but startling electric shock, and was fired when the local superintendent received the Van Horne hot foot. After a succession of training positions with small railroads, Van Horne was promoted in 1870 to be superintendent of telegraphs for the Chicago & Alton.

He married Lucy Adeline Hurd in 1866. She was a civil engineer's daughter whose beauty had won her the right to read the city's welcoming address when Abraham Lincoln visited Joliet during one of his election tours. While Van Horne was general manager of the St. Louis, Kansas City & Northern (a Chicago & Alton subsidiary) Lucy came down with smallpox. Rather than send her to the municipal pesthouse, the only provision for such cases, he moved her to the attic and alone nursed her through the day, working at night so that none of his staff would be infected.

He resigned from the Chicago & Alton in 1874 to bring the Southern Minnesota Railroad out of receivership. As president of a railway—although it was only 167 miles long and almost bankrupt—he was free for the first time to apply his imagination without the hindrance of conservative seniors. During his first year of management, operating expenses dropped from 72 to 56 per cent of earnings. He ordered free lunches for employees and personally dictated the menus. His was the first railroad to subsidize farmers who settled along its tracks.

When a grasshopper plague threatened the crops of his settlers, he developed horse-drawn sheet-iron pans smeared with tar to kill the insects. "Praying won't move one grasshopper," he told groups of farmers who were calling upon a higher agent than Van Horne for reprieve. "What you've got to do is take your coats off and hustle!" Most of the crop was saved and carried away on Van Horne's trains.

During his next job as general superintendent of the much larger Chicago, Milwaukee & St. Paul, he met James Jerome Hill, a stock promoter from Guelph, Ont., whose Great Northern later made him one of America's most important railway builders. Hill was a partner with Donald Smith and George Stephen in the St. Paul, Minneapolis & Manitoba running into Winnipeg. From Hill, Van Horne first heard the details of the great railroad enterprise being planned in Canada—then a blank area on U.S. maps, marked "British Possessions".

The first paragraph of the 1871 pact which brought British Columbia into Confederation stated that the west coast must within ten years be linked with the rest of Canada by a railway. The only existing trans-Rockies passage was by pack-horse. The lines of animals met at Punch Bowl, near what is now Jasper, Alta., to transfer loads and passengers. Captain Richard Palliser, the English engineer, declared after four years of surveying that a railway could never pierce the mountain range.

Because of changes in government policy and the Allan scandal, only two hundred miles of the trans-continental railroad had been built by February, 1881, when Donald Smith, George Stephen and James Hill incorporated the Canadian Pacific Railway Company.

"Van Horne," Hill insisted, "is the only man for the construction job—he's the best equipped mentally, and every other way." Smith and Stephen interviewed him, and agreed.

Van Horne arrived in Winnipeg on the last day of 1881; it was forty below, and a searing Arctic-born wind obstructed even across-the-street visibility. He set up his headquarters and began one of history's toughest construction jobs. Van Horne's assignment was to lay twenty-nine hundred miles of track across a barely explored continent. Two governments had spent millions of dollars during a decade of attempts to build the railway, but less than three hundred miles had been completed. The C.P.R. itself had managed to lay only a hundred miles during the 1881 construction season.

The railroad's staff of British engineers resented the intrusion of the fat Yankee with the big cigar who cursed like a spike driver and handled his subordinates with the subtlety of a starving wolfhound chasing a herd of sheep. "We did not like him when he first came to Winnipeg as general boss of everything and everybody," J. H. E. Secretan, a senior C.P.R. engineer, wrote in his diary. "His ways were not our ways . . . he told me that if he could only teach the section men to run a transit, he wouldn't have a single damn engineer about the place."

Van Horne boldly announced he would lay five hundred miles of track in 1882. By train, boat, and wagon and on horseback, he ranged the Prairies—firing, hiring, commanding. Before the ice was out of Lake Superior, rails from England and Germany were arriving in Winnipeg via New

Orleans. "Van Horne *looks* harmless," remarked the admiring *Winnipeg Sun*. "But so does a buzz saw."

Snow was still on the ground when ten thousand men and seventeen hundred teams of horses began to push Van Horne's rails westward two, three and even four miles a day —once as much as twenty miles in three days. Van Horne set a pace which kept the graders only a few miles behind the locating engineers. When the Blackfoot Indians tore up the tracks in angry night raids, Van Horne presented a lifetime C.P.R. pass to Crowfoot, their chief, with a warning not to steal any more rails if he wanted to live to use it.

By the end of the season 417 miles of main track were operating. There remained the difficult Rockies and Lake Superior sections.

The C.P.R. charter stipulated its road would cross the mountains through Yellowhead Pass, the route recommended by Sir Sandford Fleming and seven other engineers. Van Horne inspected the suggested path, and then made his own decision. "Those surveys," he announced, "will no doubt prove of great value to future alpinists. But I'm building a railroad." He picked instead the more southerly Kicking Horse Pass.

When construction was held up by an engineer's refusal to drive his locomotive over a swaying trestle, Van Horne clambered into the cab himself. "Well, if you ain't afraid of getting killed, with all your money, I ain't afraid either," reasoned the abashed engineer.

"We'll have a double funeral—at my expense, of course!" Van Horne shouted back across the wavering cab. They got across safely.

VAN HORNE 81

While his gangs were blasting the double path of iron through the mountains, Van Horne turned his energies to the even tougher construction problem of the Lake Superior link.

When the C.P.R. syndicate was formed, Hill and Smith agreed that the Superior section could not produce profitable traffic. Instead of building the C.P.R. around the northern shore of the lake they decided to put in a spur line running into a branch of the St. Paul, Minneapolis & Manitoba at Sault Ste. Marie. "Using Mr. Hill's line," Van Horne protested to the directors, "plainly puts the mighty C.P.R. at his tender mercies."

With added pressure from Sir John A. Macdonald, who wanted to keep the road entirely on Canadian soil, the majority of the company directors backed down. Hill immediately resigned from the C.P.R. board, sold his shares, and launched a paid smear campaign against the securities on American stock exchanges. "I'll get Van Horne," he vowed, "if I have to go to hell for it and shovel coal." Years later Hill's Great Northern still would not sell through tickets to passengers who wanted to board C.P.R. steamers to the Orient.

Van Horne toured the north shore of Lake Superior and returned with a typical conclusion. "It's two hundred miles of engineering impossibility," he reported. "But we'll bridge it."

The Superior shore is a land half drowned in its own juices —a jungle of muskeg, matted quicksand and stunted spruce forests. Van Horne's accomplishment in carving a railroad through this soggy wilderness was a breath-taking lesson in the rearrangement of geography.

Van Horne decided to build the tracks near the shore-line, so that construction could be supplied by water. He imported Clyde-built steamers to plant caches of materials. To reduce haulage he built factories in the bush that turned out three tons of dynamite a day. By the spring of 1884, nine thousand men were working in the swamps. One particularly bitter stretch of muskeg cost $750,000 to cross. It swallowed the track seven times, along with three locomotives. Between Sudbury and Cartier a lake had to be lowered ten feet to get a foundation for track, and three miles of curved track were needed to go around Jackfish Bay, although the jump across was only half a mile.

The formidable convulsions of nature which had fashioned Superior's shore were only one of Van Horne's worries in 1884. C.P.R. financing through the sale of common stock was lagging badly due to opposition lobbies and pressure from European financiers who had lost heavily on other railway ventures. Construction crews went for months without a pay-car on the sidings.

When creditors came to Van Horne, he almost always managed to postpone the bills. "Go sell your boots and buy C.P.R. stock!" was his inevitable parting sally. In Parliament, Liberals charged that for six months of the year, the railroad would be "an idle, ice-bound, snow-covered route." Opposition leader Edward Blake predicted the mountain section "would not pay for the grease on the axles."

Van Horne was infuriated by newspaper criticism. He wrote the editor of the *Manitoba Free Press*: "I think you are the damndest—I was going to say the damndest fool I've ever known, but I can't say that, because I've known two or three others who completed their record by dying in their foolishness, while your record is still incomplete, and there is a fair chance that you may yet make a turn and come to an end under suspicion of having had some sense."

Van Horne attracted controversy. The C.P.R. charter named Port Moody as the road's western terminal. But dissatisfied with harbour facilities there, Van Horne chose instead a spot on Burrard Inlet. He named it Vancouver after the British captain who landed there in 1792. The settlement had previously been known as Gastown, after Gassy Jack Deighton, a local hotel-keeper. There was loud agitation to have it called Granville, for Great Britain's colonial secretary. "Hell," declared Van Horne, "this isn't going to be the kind of town you name after an absentee governor."

The C.P.R. often recalled Van Horne from the West to help with the necessarily frequent assaults on the federal treasury for more construction loans. In the winter of 1885, Sir John A. Macdonald had just flatly denied the promoters another cent when word reached Ottawa that the fanatic, Louis Riel, was back recruiting the disenchanted *métis* who now hated the C.P.R. as much as they had once despised the Hudson's Bay Company.

Van Horne reminded the Prime Minister that it had taken him ninety days to get troops from Toronto to Winnipeg during the first revolt. "Put two batteries of men in my care," he told Macdonald, "and I guarantee to have them on the Qu'Appelle in eleven days." Macdonald, who had the day before been told that the railroad must have more money to bridge the many gaps in its line north of Superior, was skeptical—but the only alternative was to wait for spring breakup, and by then Riel could have the uprising effectively organized.

Forty-eight hours after Macdonald agreed to try the scheme, Van Horne's trains pulled into Ottawa to load the troops. Singing *The Girl I Left Behind Me,* the soldiers marched to the station for the most remarkable ride in Canadian military history. At each end of steel, Van Horne packed them on freight sleds. Trains were routed across frozen rivers on tracks laid only hours before. The portage operation halted twice a day for warm chicken or steak dinners, supplied by the company on Van Horne's orders. The first contingent reached Winnipeg in four days. The revolt was dispersed and Riel hanged at Regina. The army was still in the field when Macdonald agreed to grant the loan which financed the final stretch of C.P.R. construction.

The last C.P.R. rail was laid at 9.22 A.M. on November 7, 1885, at Craigellachie, B.C. That afternoon Donald Smith hammered in the last spike.

Van Horne stood at his right elbow, unsmiling but obviously pleased. He had arrived in Canada forty-six months before. Behind him stretched twin ribbons of steel, 2,905 miles long. To show off his railway, Van Horne shortly afterwards bet a group of newspapermen he could run them the 840 miles from Winnipeg to the Rocky foothills between dawn and dusk. He made it, but to shorten the odds he chose to make the trip on June 21, the longest day of the year.

Completion of the main line meant that Van Horne could begin to shape the C.P.R. into an integrated transportation network. Named to succeed Stephen as President on August 7, 1888, he immediately expanded the company's colonization program. He offered free homes in the West for teachers and doctors.

To boost the quality of prairie grain he built a million-bushel elevator at Fort William. His critics claimed the entire West would never grow enough wheat to fill it. He put the company into the wheat business, and offered half a dollar per bushel while brokers were bidding thirty-five cents. When a delegation of Manitoba farmers demanded lower freight rates, he dismissed them with the shout: "Raise less hell and more wheat!" Ironically, he turned down suggestions by Thomas Shaughnessy, his assistant manager, that the C.P.R. should drill for oil in Alberta. Such a venture, he insisted, would be hopeless.

"Since we can't export the scenery, we'll import the tourists," he told his assistants, and mapped out Canada's first major tourist campaign. He put up a string of hotels, including the Chateau Frontenac at Quebec City and the Chateau Lake Louise, facing the Victoria Glacier. Then he hired artists to paint their pictures inside every C.P.R. sleeping car. He wrote most of the company's advertising slogans himself, producing such bizarre legends as "WISE MEN OF THE EAST, GO WEST BY C.P.R.", and "BY THUNDER! (BAY) PASSES THE C.P.R.!" When he opened the new Windsor Station in Montreal, his ads proudly announced, "BEATS ALL CREATION, THAT C.P.R. STATION!"

Van Horne ran his railroad with the flair of a circus barker who knows he's fronting the fair's best show. Quickly bored with head office routine, he ranged over the system, making drastic improvements on the spot. He was thought by many trainmen to have the powers of the devil himself. One of the incidents which established him in this category began as he was tramping up and down the Sudbury station platform, waiting for his train to start. Bundled into his winter furs he went unrecognized. As he passed the caboose, he overheard the brakeman boasting about the sleep he got on his run. When he reached Montreal, Van Horne discovered the negligent trainman's name and dispatched a telegram to the train's conductor: "GO INTO THE CABOOSE AND YOU WILL FIND JOHN ROGERS ASLEEP WAKE HIM AND SHOW HIM THIS TELEGRAM—VAN HORNE". The frightened brakeman told and retold the story so effectively that C.P.R. train crews from then on did their dozing off the job.

The frequent exercise of Van Horne's formidable memory gave him a reputation for second sight. One evening at Government House in Ottawa, he met an English engineer who had just returned from Japan. After a few drinks, the Englishman casually told the guests that his wife, who was still in the Orient, had allowed a tattoo artist to imprint a life-size bluebottle on the upper part of her left arm. A year later at a Montreal dinner, Van Horne was introduced to the engineer's wife, who had come to the dinner alone, and he immediately recalled the name and the tattoo story. Having heard about his reputation for mind reading, she demanded, "Sir William, tell me, what am I thinking of?" After a prolonged pretence of reluctance, Van Horne agreed to perform the experiment. He asked that the lights be lowered, looked at her in profound concentration. Then with eyes closed, he intoned: "You are thinking of something alive . . . an insect, perhaps . . . you are thinking of the picture of a bluebottle tattooed on your arm." He poked his finger at the spot just as the brash young lady fainted. Van Horne would only shrug when the other guests demanded that he explain his feat.

He aimed many of his practical jokes at the stuffier members of the C.P.R. board with cruel disregard for their comfort. During an inspection tour of the Rockies, he stopped the train, with the suggestion that Sir William Peterson, a C.P.R. director and principal of McGill University, might be interested in some "Indian statues" at a nearby gorge. While the professor was poking around the "statues"—which turned out to be piles of rocks left over from construction— Van Horne ordered the train to start. Peterson was nearly injured jumping onto the accelerating last coach, as Van Horne cheered him on, smacking his large thighs in glee.

He was a good billiard shot despite his girth and a master chess player, but his favourite relaxation was poker—a pastime he referred to as "not a game, but an education." On one journey from Winnipeg to Montreal, he could find no partners, so he commandeered the conductor—then promptly fired him at Fort William, because he had recently issued a warning that no employee was to engage in cards while on duty. When he returned to Montreal, however, he moved the disgraced man to a better job at head office. Van Horne gave away most of his considerable poker winnings to hospitals, in the names of those partners who rarely made any charitable contributions. He would send the donors' lists to the newspapers and anonymously mail clippings to the indignant gamesters.

Another favourite exercise in buffoonery was his cigar prank. A firm of cut-rate tobacconists had capitalized on his fame by calling a five-cent brand "The Van Horne". He ordered hundreds of the leafy horrors, removed their bands, mixed them into his humidor with expensive perfectos, and then palmed them off on his guests. His visitors, wishing to acknowledge his reputation as a connoisseur, would inhale the tarry mixture, and exclaim : "Ah, Sir William, what a delightful aroma!" They could only smile icily at Van Horne's crude guffaw which followed his explanation. He once hired a man simply because he had butted one of the dud cigars and asked, "How much does the stable boy charge you for these things?"

Such amusements provided Van Horne with only minor diversion. His serious interest in art occupied most of his spare time, but he also loved the symphonies of Beethoven and often read a book in a night. He had no patience with authors who analyzed the moral reasoning of their characters. "I want something doing," he told a McGill English professor, "I don't care a rap *why* people do things in novels or real life. Working out motives is about as useful as a signboard on Niagara Falls." He considered collectors of first editions *poseurs*. "Give me a book for use," he insisted. "If the margins are too wide, cut them down. If the covers are too clumsy, tear them off. If you buy a book as a work of art, throw it in your cabinet and order a modern edition for reading."

Van Horne's study was hung with fifteenth-century ship models. He had one of the largest collections of Japanese pottery in North America and two hundred paintings, which even during his lifetime were valued at more than three million dollars. Velvet wall hangings provided the mellow backdrop for the works he owned of Rubens, Titian, Magnasco, Murillo, Velasquez, El Greco, Renoir, Reynolds, Hogarth, Turner and Courbet. He had four Rembrandts, two Goyas, four Franz Hals, and a da Vinci study of a woman's head—the character and proportions of her face resembling those of the "Mona Lisa." (Part of the collection was sold after his death and part was given to the Montreal Museum of Fine Arts by his granddaughter. But the greatest number of paintings, including the most valuable canvases, remains locked in Van Horne's home, now seen only by the widow of his last grandson, who lives there alone.)

To expand his collection Van Horne often attended the auction marts of London and Paris, bidding because he considered paintings inherently good or bad. "The purchase of a picture is like the selection of a wife," he maintained. "Never buy one that you don't fall in love with."

Van Horne's astounding knowledge of Japanese pottery was recognized by museum experts on four continents. He could identify nine out of ten Oriental ceramic objects while blindfolded, naming the long extinct kilns where they had been fired. To illustrate a privately published catalogue of his collection, he produced a hundred watercolour sketches of the best pieces.

When he was showing an admiring guest through his gallery, Van Horne would pause before a gaudy landscape signed "Henri Rousseau"—a French primitive artist who was very popular during the last quarter of the nineteenth century. He would wait for his visitor to mouth the appropriate flattery on his taste in art, then declare with a slap of the visitor's back that he had painted the canvas himself.

His lack of technique marred many of his pictures, but his drawing was good—especially the anatomy of trees—and his sense of colour was professionally true. He once painted a canvas a day for three months, working until two or three o'clock in the morning. During his European tours he would send postcards home with watercolour sketches of his activities, depicting himself as an elephant. His best paintings were "Moonlight on the St. Croix River"—a beautiful sea and cloud composition—"The Birch", and "Steel Mills in Nova Scotia at Night".

These canvases were completed in his studio on top of a specially erected outlook tower at "Covenhoven", his sprawling summer home on thousand-acre Minister's Island in Passamaquoddy Bay. The estate had its own vineyards and peach orchards. Because Van Horne didn't consider peaches fit to eat until they dropped off the trees, the fruit fell into soft nets rigged below each branch. In his greenhouse, he developed a triple trumpet flower at a time when only a few doubles had been successfully cultivated.

He raised acres of mushrooms and became an expert at identifying hundreds of varieties. In an interview with the managing director of *The Times,* Moberly Bell, he solemnly observed : "Most toadstool victims are buried on Wednesday. They inevitably pick the spurious mushrooms on Sunday walks, have them for supper, and die just in time to be decently interred by midweek."

The living-room of this summer home, later rented to an American senator, was so large that it took eight men to lift the Indian rug he bought to cover the floor. The room's twenty-foot granite fireplace was flanked by ornately carved Italian pillars, covered in gold leaf.

He owned a four-thousand-acre farm near Selkirk, Man., where he grew wheat and raised prize cattle, but a fifty-two-room house at 1139 Sherbrooke Street West in Montreal was his main home. A depressing three-story Victorian baronial mansion built like an armoury, its most attractive room was his study—half of an upstairs floor crammed with ship models and Oriental curios.

Van Horne preferred to deal with company matters in his C.P.R. presidential office on the fifth floor of the Windsor Station. He faced his callers—no matter how eminent—straddling his armless chair backwards as if on a saddle. He would rest his elbows on his stomach, which was propped against the chair's stiff back. When he became excited he would kick the chair over. His assistants learned to expect the unexpected. He once dictated a burning memorandum that any C.P.R. engineer caught in a race with competing Canada Atlantic trains would be fired at once. Then he called his secretary back to add a footnote: "Any C.P.R. engineer who allows a Canada Atlantic train to beat him shall also be liable for instant dismissal."

He internationalized the C.P.R.'s operations by building a fleet of ocean liners. His *Empress of India* offered history's first round-the-world cruises under the flag of a single company. He also took time out to design the red-and-white house flag of the C.P.R.'s steamships. He drafted construction plans for thirty-thousand-passenger transatlantic ferries, but his directors turned down the scheme. The $21 million, triple-hulled steamers, laid out with avenues, cafés and theatres, were to have been built in the Bay of Fundy by damming up one of its inlets.

Van Horne became so nationalistic that he eventually renounced his American citizenship. "To have built that road," he said, "would have made a Canadian out of the German Emperor." On a tour of Europe he touted the glorious future of Canada as being certain as the sunrise.

He startled many people on both sides of the border when he told a visiting U.S. senator: "I am a Chinese Wall protectionist. I don't mean merely in trade. I mean everything. I'd keep American ideas out of this country."

As his adopted country's greatest railroad builder, Van Horne contributed more significantly to the evolution of the Canadian economy than any other American.

Asked twice by Sir John A. Macdonald to accept a knighthood, Van Horne finally yielded in 1895. He became the first non-British subject to wear the knight's cross of the order of St. Michael and St. George. On the morning his appointment was announced, the Windsor Station doorman, who customarily greeted him with a friendly wave, bowed and said, "Good morning, Sir William." Van Horne shouted "OH HELL!" at the startled fellow, and would see no one for the rest of the morning. He refused to accept any of the honorary university degrees offered him, because he believed degrees should be awarded for academic achievement only.

When the 1899 recession temporarily halted the C.P.R.'s expansion, Van Horne decided to resign. As soon as the rumour reached traders on the New York and London exchanges, they expressed their regard for his ability by selling off C.P.R. stock so sharply that quotations dropped ten points.

Conservative politicians urged him to stand for office, but Van Horne was not interested. "Nothing could induce me to go into politics," he declared. "I would as soon think of becoming a parson." Reluctantly he agreed to take a holiday in Mexico. "I got as far as Monterrey," he said later. "I went out on the verandah, sat down and smoked a big cigar. Then

I got up, and looked at the scenery. It was very fine. Then I sat down again and smoked another cigar. Then I jumped up, and telephoned for my car to be coupled to the next train, and by jinks, I was never so happy in my life, as when I struck the C.P.R. again."

His daily contacts with the C.P.R. ended when he resigned, but Van Horne always championed the road, urging all his friends to buy its stock. He predicted in 1899 that the company's shares would hit $206 by 1910 and lived to see them climb fifty points higher.

Even Van Horne's magnificent optimism could never have visualized his railroad's rise to its present status—representing a capital investment of $3 billion yielding net profits of $50 million a year. As well as seventeen thousand miles of track in Canada, and another four thousand miles in the U.S., the company operates the world's seventh largest airline and major steamship interests. Its Consolidated Mining & Smelting Company owns the richest lead and zinc mine in the world. It runs Canada's largest hotel chain, holds a million acres of oil and mineral rights, operates meat-packing plants, bus and truck lines, Turkish baths, dance halls and the Western Hemisphere's biggest glass-covered salt-water swimming pool.

Van Horne was rescued from his restlessness following his break with the C.P.R. by American investors who asked him to take over electrification of Havana streetcars, at that time pulled by mules. With his usual foresight, Van Horne quickly reached beyond the city's problems and became interested in the island's railroads. Cuba had 1,135 miles of track, nearly all of it around Havana; the sugar-rich eastern provinces could be reached only by water. Van Horne took a ten-day horseback journey through the interior and decided to span the island with a railroad. His name was so well established that he lined up the necessary $8 million financing during a five-day visit to New York.

Location surveys began from Santa Clara in July, 1900. To cut freight costs, Van Horne instructed his gangs to make bridges and trestles out of local materials. One foreman took the orders so literally that he made a bridge out of expensive mahogany, the timber nearest the site. The line was completed December 1, 1902; crossing the island had been reduced from a ten-day hardship to a one-day excursion. To bolster the road's traffic, Van Horne converted an old government barracks at Camaguey into a modern hotel. Two years later he helped build the trans-Guatemala railway, but it became profitable only a decade after his death.

His C.P.R. presidency had brought Van Horne many investment opportunities in Canada. He became associated in a major way with the modernization of the Toronto, Saint John and Winnipeg tramway systems, and in 1892, established the Windsor Salt Company. He was President of the Laurentide Pulp Company, controlling large timber tracts around the St. Maurice River, and built a pulp mill at Grand Falls in New Brunswick. He was a vice-president and major shareholder of the Dominion Iron & Steel Company at Sydney, N.S. During the first decade of this century, his position on the boards of thirty-three major corporations made him one of Canada's most influential business men.

Not all his ventures were successful. He lost his entire investment in the Horsefly & Cariboo Hydraulic Mining Company, a placer gold mining operation in B.C. His fish cannery near his summer home cost him $200,000 before he abandoned the experiment.

Van Horne was seventy-one when World War I was declared. Sensing that victory to a large degree would depend on the Allies' ability in hunting the Kaiser's submarines, he invented a magnetic detection device. The British Admiralty, which was then experimenting, among other gimmicks, with the training of sea lions to spot submarines, rejected his invention without a trial. Similar principles but improved methods were adopted by the anti-submarine squadrons of the U.S. and Canadian navies in 1950.

Van Horne had never seen war, but he regarded battle as an essential catalyst for the development of man's best qualities. "If universal peace were brought about, I feel sure it would result in universal rottenness," he said in a Canadian Club speech.

He also philosophized about the roots of his full life. "Some of us get impressions," he said, "vivid impressions, which call for our industry. This industry leads to facility, and everything becomes easy."

Shortly before his death, he summarized for a Montreal friend the simple philosophy which had guided his remarkable life. With typical Van Horne optimism, he expressed himself in the present tense: "I eat all I can, I drink all I can, I smoke all I can and I don't give a damn for anything."

chapter 4

SIR JAMES DUNN

*He became rich at a time when
wealth naturally kindled arrogance. He won personal power
when there were few barriers
either to its acquisition or its use.*

No career in Canadian business history has been masked more completely by the colourful tunic of legend than the life of Sir James Hamet Dunn, the carpenter's son from Bathurst, N.B., who became this country's most flamboyant multi-millionaire.

Dunn had all the assets and all the liabilities of a promoter. A totally self-made man and disproportionately proud of it, he became rich at a time when wealth naturally kindled arrogance. He won personal power when there were few barriers either to its acquisition or its use.

His princely habits were the spicy gossip of an envious generation. Less well known were Dunn's astute mastery of international finance and his instinct for profitable corporation management.

A multi-millionaire by the time he was thirty-nine, Dunn was one of the most garish spenders of his age. But during his lifetime few recognized him as the man who succeeded in Canada's most daring industrial coup—a scheme, nurtured through a quarter century of patient and deliberate planning, which delivered into his control the $75 million Algoma Steel Corporation for an investment of under $10 million.

Dunn's whip-stiff management transformed the cold, promoter-drained Algoma into the second-largest and most profitable steel producer in the country. The stock market reflected accurately the spectacular efficiency of his rule : Algoma common shares, which hovered around a doubtful $74 when Dunn took over in 1935, were worth the equivalent of $375 when he died.

Yet Algoma shareholders supplied Dunn's strangest obituary. They were so delighted with the news of his death that on January 3, 1956, the first market day after his fatal stroke, their extra buying pushed Algoma shares an astounding $16.75 over the closing quote of the day when Dunn still ruled the empire that he had laboured so brilliantly to create.

This was partly the result of long frustration over Dunn's insistence that profits should go into capital expansion rather than dividends. But more than that, the market's action reflected profound relief that the affairs of Algoma had finally passed out of the hands of a man who might be envied, but who could not be understood.

Hampered only by the vagaries of his impulses, Dunn appeared to the world as a determinate eccentric. His waspish insistence on his own way in all things, regardless of the number of enemies it might make him, had an upsetting effect on the cautiously conforming less extraordinary Canadians of his day.

Annoyed by a railway steward's manners or by the preparation of his order, Dunn would tear the cloth off the table, dumping his dinner to the floor. At airports he often grabbed the reservation desk telephone to place private calls and to bellow out orders to his subordinates. His favourite suit was white serge, worn with a white shirt and set off by a pillar-box red necktie.

During supper in a Riviera restaurant Dunn once demanded a certain kind of cracker with his cheese. When he was told that it wasn't stocked he phoned Canada to have three cases flown over the same night. Because he was displeased with the chef's cooking and the colour of the dinnerware at the Windsor Hotel in Sault Ste. Marie, he purchased the nine-storey structure and hired a new kitchen staff. Then he had the window of his top-floor suite enlarged so that he might survey the 2,300 acres of the city and four miles of waterfront which were his own. Because of repeated airport delays, Dunn also bought Sault Ste. Marie's transportation system and a fleet of taxis. He later sold both at a profit. Algoma still owns the hotel.

Verdicts of Dunn's accomplishments varied widely. "Algoma Steel, which testifies to his own personal endeavour, has lost the greatest man it will ever know," said David Holbrook, Dunn's successor. "We have surely passed beyond the day when wealth could be equated with greatness," editorialized the *Toronto Star*. "It is not really known whether Dunn's charity exceed his self-indulgence, for he lived in kingly style."

Dunn's private fortune at times exceeded $100 million. His spectacular opulence showed up in his distaste for all smokes except the cucumber-size cigars specially rolled for him in Cuba, at a dollar each. He had a private brand of whisky blended in Scotland, with his name on the label of every bottle. When the five-thousand-dollar Persian poodle he had bought his wife became ill in New Brunswick, Dunn ordered a veterinarian flown in from Montreal. In his libraries, one of the world's most valuable private book collections was dispersed among canvases by Salvador Dali, Fra Filippo Lippi and Sir William Orpen.

His reverence for wealth made him reject large-scale charity. He believed that handouts kept people from working. But he did support substantially hospitals in Sault Ste. Marie and St. Andrews, N.B., and his gifts to universities— particularly Dalhousie and the University of New Brunswick —were recognized with six honorary degrees. His public replies at these presentations constituted nearly the total of Dunn's speeches. One of the talks was a lyrical salute to his Celtic heritage. "The Celt loves to dream, and God bless him for it. His are not the thin vapourings of the idle mind, but rather the vision of a busy brain; the kind of dreams that open new frontiers and build for greatness," he told a graduating class at St. Francis Xavier University of Antigonish, N.S., an institution that he supported despite its anti-capitalist teachings.

Dunn was in his most stimulating mood as an after-dinner raconteur. His story-telling skill prompted Lord Beaverbrook to classify him "among the very few men of great business affairs recognized for their conversational powers."

The mercurial Dunn had difficulty containing his temperament within the same walls for any extended period. He loved to dash off across the Atlantic unexpectedly in the best cabins of the best liners. For local travel he maintained a fleet of four private airplanes—two DC-3's, furnished as flying offices, a Beechcraft and a Norseman. When the weather delayed his departure, Dunn would hire a private railway car from the C.P.R.

Rented quarters could never quite keep pace with his whims. In Toronto, for instance, Dunn at first stayed in the vice-regal suite of the Royal York. But when the hotel banned Lady Dunn's dogs, he transferred to the King Edward. After a row with the management there, he moved temporarily into a private sitting-room of the Toronto General Hospital.

Dunn's favourite residence was "Dayspring", his turreted manor-house at St. Andrews, on the shore of Passamaquoddy Bay, bought for $230,000 from I. E. Smoot, the Washington sand-and-gravel magnate. Surrounded by an eight-foot wooden fence fronted with a thick cedar hedge, the cream-coloured mansion had thirty rooms, five fireplaces, an air-conditioned theatre and the country's best wine cellar.

Permanent households were also maintained by Dunn on a smaller but equally luxurious scale at Jamestown, near the Algoma mine, in England and in France. The French home was a two-storey villa at Cap Ferrat on the Riviera. The London headquarters was purchased for $145,000 from the Rt. Hon. Reginald McKenna, a former chancellor of the

Exchequer. For maximum seclusion, Dunn retired to a 1,700-acre hunting estate near Bathurst, N.B.

His insistence on palatial surroundings reflected Dunn's efforts to compensate for the oppressive poverty of his childhood. He was born in 1875 to a Bathurst woodworker thrown out of work by the decline of the sailing ships. After he graduated from St. Peter's Village School, young Jimmy became a clerk in the office of George Gilbert, the town lawyer. During a legal errand to Chatham, fifty miles away, he made friends with Dick Bennett and Max Aitken, clerks in the law office of L. J. Tweedie. Bennett later became Canada's fifteenth prime minister; Aitken, as Lord Beaverbrook, eventually wielded the greatest backstage political power of any publisher in history.

Dunn became discouraged by his lack of prospects in the Maritimes and when he was eighteen, moved to Lynn, Mass., as an armature winder in an electrical works. Shortly afterwards, he won ten dollars in the prize ring for knocking down a circus boxer. He used part of the money to get a ticket for the local lecture by "Professor Loisette", inventor of the so-called assimilative memory method—a clever parlour trick exhibition of mind reading. Dunn was so impressed by the lecturer that he joined his troupe as advance booking agent for a tour of the U.S. and England. The "Professor" wanted to take the hustling Jimmy on his junket to India as well, but the youngster decided instead to spend his savings of $650 on gaining a law degree from Dalhousie University.

To supplement the finances for his education Dunn spent the summers as a Halifax tugboat deck-hand. He is remembered at Dalhousie more for his rebellious questioning of the lecturers than for academic achievements. When Professor Benjamin Russell (later a Nova Scotia Supreme Court judge) gave a legal interpretation in the class dealing with property law, Dunn jumped up and declared, "Lord Eldon, with whom I agree, has a different opinion."

Dunn left Halifax in 1898, the day after he was admitted to the provincial bar, as the agent for a group of Maritimers who held the charter to construct a railway from Edmonton to the Yukon. In Edmonton, Dunn soon realized that the railroad could not be built without a federal amendment to provide for a branch line as far as the Pacific coast. His newly established law office had few customers and made little money. When a client asked him to name his fee for representing him in a federal Department of the Interior hearing for overland route operations north of Edmonton, Dunn asked only for the price of a one-way ticket to Ottawa. He never returned to the Prairies.

After settling that case, Dunn obtained the amendment which made the Edmonton–Yukon charter interesting enough for sale to the Mackenzie and Mann railway syndicate. Soon he was appearing before many parliamentary committees, particularly as the representative of corporations seeking federal charters. He usually acquired part of their stock as his fee. His eloquence was noticed by J. N. Greenshields, the Montreal stockbroker, who made him a junior partner. His own stock, and contacts made through his marriage to Gertrude Price, a Quebec City heiress, provided him with such good backing that he gradually switched from law to international finance.

His first marriage lasted twenty-five years. He was divorced in 1926 to marry the lively Marchioness of Queensberry, a popular member of Europe's international set which then included the present Duke of Windsor. Sixteen years after his second marriage, Dunn was divorced again. His last wife was Marcia Christoforides. He had hired her as a secretary after meeting her in Lord Beaverbrook's office at the *Daily Express*.

Following his first marriage, Dunn bought a seat on the Montreal Stock Exchange with a borrowed $20,000. Many wealthy Canadians were then using bank loans to acquire large blocks of securities in South American railroads and power companies. Dunn made his initial fortune by creating a public market in Canada and Britain for these stocks. One of his first big deals was the sale of a million dollars' worth of Havana Electric Company bonds to British buyers.

He moved to England in 1905 and two years later with a partner established Dunn, Fisher & Company, a private underwriting house. He eventually bought out his partner and expanded to the continent. By 1914, at thirty-nine, he was a multi-millionaire and recognized as a major influence in trans-Atlantic finance.

Dunn's firm underwrote many South American enterprises for Canadian clients, retaining control in this country of such enterprises as Mexico Tramways and Mexican Light & Power Company. Over a Paris luncheon table, Dunn worked out the details of the triple utilities merger which resulted in the formation during 1912 of Brazilian Traction, Light & Power Company. He also was one of the major backers of the Barcelona Traction, Light & Power Company, which still operates in northern and eastern Spain.

During the five years before World War I, Dunn's firm was buying and selling each day securities worth $10 million and earning its owner a daily commission of about $60,000. Otto Kahn, the famous American banker, called Dunn "a greater financier than all of us."

The outbreak of war sharply altered the direction of Dunn's career. By a series of immensely intricate manoeuvres he was able to obtain control for the British Government of nickel deposits in Norway, thus halting the flow of the vital element from neutral Europe into Germany. His services were repaid with a baronetcy on George V's 1921 honours list.

Because World War I ended most British financing of foreign enterprises, Dunn began to raise funds for domestic corporations. His most successful undertaking was the merger of England's major tile manufacturers into the Marley Tile Company.

Despite his involvement in world finances, the self-exiled Dunn never lost interest in Canada. Ever since Francis Hector Clergue had conducted him on a tour of the Algoma country near Sault Ste. Marie in 1907, he had been quietly buying up the low-priced bonds of the Algoma Steel Corporation.

Clergue had come to Lake Superior in 1893 for a Philadelphia group interested in harnessing undeveloped water resources. He surveyed the Soo rapids cascading out of Lake Superior and decided to utilize part of their energy by putting up a power house on the St. Mary's River. The financial panic of the late nineties left him with so much unsold power that he built a sawmill to put it to work, and then found he had to provide a railway to haul his logs. During the road's construction, iron ore deposits were found. The discovery prompted Clergue to purchase and move in an abandoned steel mill from Ohio. In the decade of Clergue's stewardship, Sault Ste. Marie became a Canadian Pittsburgh. He invested more than $100 million in machine shops, foundries, blast furnaces, development of the mines and completion of the 106-mile Algoma Central & Hudson Bay Railway.

But the company's too heavy emphasis on turning out rails at a time when most of the country's main railways had been completed gradually weakened its position. When an American railroad rejected an order of Algoma rails because of their too great carbon content, the company—whose reserves and profits were already committed to future projects —was badly hit. The Royal Canadian Regiment had to be called in from Toronto to quell employees rioting for their wages. Clergue's dream was declared bankrupt in 1907.

Dunn was hired as one of the liquidators of the derelict empire. Part of his job was to wind up the Sovereign Bank which had made large loans to the Canadian Improvement Company, formed by Clergue to underwrite the bonds of his Lake Superior Corporation. He interested Robert Fleming, the British financier, in the situation and with him purchased $25 million worth of Algoma's five per cent first and refunding bonds at a New York auction for slightly more than $6 million. Dunn acquired Fleming's securities in 1925. Following its first bankruptcy, Algoma had to meet the interest on those bonds out of its capital account. By 1932 its current-asset account had been depleted and Algoma's funded debt per ton of ingot capacity amounted to $47.74 compared with $16.41 at the Steel Company of Canada.

On August 13, 1932, the blast furnaces were allowed to cool and the plant was closed. Algoma's second bankruptcy was triggered by its inability to pay a coal bill for $62,476 to the Cannelton Coal & Coke Company, a subsidiary. A new Algoma Steel Corporation was organized two years later. The owners of the first mortgage bonds were issued common shares in the new company; holders of old common stock got nothing. Dunn, who had by then collected about 80 per cent of the bonds, thus acquired more than three-quarters of the controlling common shares.

Although Dunn had initially been attracted to Algoma by its speculative possibilities, he now took over personal direction of its operations. Aided by a large rail order from the Federal Government (then headed by his old friend R. B. Bennett) he converted the starved shell of the company into the country's most efficiently operated steel plant.

Dunn made every important corporate decision following the 1935 reorganization, but his activities were kept so secret that his name didn't appear on the Algoma annual report until 1938. During the first decade of his rule he managed to cancel the company's entire funded debt, so that by 1947 only the common stock was outstanding, with himself as its majority holder.

Algoma quickly became the lowest-cost steel producer on the continent, turning out half of Canada's pig-iron and a third of the country's steel. The financier suddenly became an apostle of steel. "All the guns in Christendom, all the planes in the sky and all the gold in the vaults of the treasury will profit us nothing, if iron ore is not available in limitless tonnages to our blast furnaces," he told the Toronto Canadian Club in 1952.

In 1951, Dunn acquired control in Canada Steamship Lines Limited, the country's largest shipping operation.

He often boasted to his friends that he would live to be a

hundred. In the last years of his life he refused to desert any of his pleasures but he did add brewer's yeast and wheat germ to his diet, practised yoga breathing techniques and experimented (briefly) with vegetarianism. He died of a stroke at his St. Andrews mansion in 1956, nineteen years short of the century mark.

Half of Dunn's $66 million estate was left to his third wife with the balance divided among his five children and a granddaughter. The government took about 48 per cent of the estate in succession duties. The sum was used to finance in part the creation of the Canada Council for the Encouragement of the Arts, Humanities and Social Sciences.

Four days after Dunn's death, the heavily brocaded gates of the St. Andrews estate swung open to release a black hearse bearing his plain mahogany casket. He was cremated in a fifteen-minute ceremony attended by nine mourners.

"Dunn had tremendous faith in himself and in Canada, and because of it left this country a tremendous inheritance," wrote the Toronto *Globe & Mail* in its obituary. "If that is eccentricity, we could well use more of it."

chapter 5

SIR HARRY OAKES

"I found the pot of gold at the end of the rainbow,
and I found it in Canada. But I was
paying out 80 per cent of the gold I'd found in taxes.
Man don't work for that."

IF achievement could tame inside a man the peremptory grip of his ambition, Sir Harry Oakes would have lived happily, died quietly and been revered by his world. Instead he spent the potentially most productive period of his life booting his millions about with selfish bitterness. When he was hacked to death in one of the century's most gruesome murders, only his family mourned.

Oakes spent twenty-five years ransacking the rind of four continents in his furious hunt for gold, and finally found a quarter-billion-dollar lode on the south shore of Kirkland

Lake, in northern Ontario. It brought him the largest fortune ever garnered by an individual from Canadian mining.

He was the only prospector in Canadian history to stake and bring into dividend-paying production a major mine without surrendering financial control. His Lake Shore became during his lifetime "the richest half mile in the world." The stock that he had peddled for $32\frac{1}{2}$ cents rocketed to $62.50 while he still held an estimated million shares.

Oakes could easily have fathered a Canadian mining complex of unprecedented scope. But he allowed instead his tremendous wealth and influence to follow in the blunt pursuit of his pleasures.

Oakes was a short (5′ 6$\frac{1}{2}$″), belligerent barrel of a man. He had a nose shaped like a half-empty tooth-paste tube, and eyes that appeared to shift in an instant from a man's expression to the motives behind it. He could not belly-laugh, even at the mistakes of others. He hated to listen, but would lecture authoritatively on every subject in almost grammatical English.

Having had to outrun rabbits for his diet during most of his life, he regarded society's manners as rules meant to be broken by those who wished to maintain their independent self-respect. He would spit seeds from his hot-house grapes across the table at dinner guests. If a dowager began to twitter at him about "his early days", he would shuffle away, whistling to himself.

Ten-cent poker was his limit. When he was still a prospector he was known among Kirkland Lake bootleggers as "One-Treat Harry"; he bought more than one drink for no man, but gladly guzzled all that others would buy.

Once wealthy, he indulged in a carousel of extravagance. He owned mansions in Niagara Falls, Bar Harbor, London, Sussex, Palm Beach and Nassau, and built himself a nine-hole golf course and a fancy *château* in Kirkland Lake, overlooking the tailings dump of his mine. He stopped his engineers from sinking a new Lake Shore shaft near his grounds, because he said it would ruin his game.

He was the most niggardly philanthropist among the rich Canadians of his time. His gifts to Kirkland Lake consisted of a church site, free skates, toboggans and Books of Knowledge for local school children and a $75,000 skating rink. When he was being conducted to the rink's opening ceremonies, a hobo asked him for a dollar. Oakes cut him down with an oath. "Why," a companion demanded, "if you are about to give away seventy-five thousand dollars, didn't you give a dollar bill to a poor misfit who probably needs it?" Oakes replied, "The rink is for the kids; men can look after themselves."

"What Harry Oakes might have done, and what he did for Kirkland Lake, which gave him its wealth, are as far apart as the poles," the *Rouyn-Noranda Press* stated in an editorial after his death.

On the other hand, Kirkland Lake did not exist when Oakes first arrived in Northern Ontario.

Spurred by the silver riches of Cobalt, discovered in 1903 during the building of the Timiskaming & Northern Ontario Railway, prospectors had followed the old Troyes Trail to find the region's first gold in narrow, high-grade veinlets fingering through the greenish dolomite on the eastern shores of Larder Lake. Twenty-six miles west of Larder, at Swastika, more ore was dug up and the first gold mill was built. But the Kirkland Lake district between Larder and Swastika was totally ignored by the rush of prospectors, more interested in the mammoth Hollinger and Dome strikes farther to the north.

Oakes heard only distant and distorted reports of the Canadian gold finds on his flax farm in New Zealand. He had put $30,000 from a small gold strike he made in Australia into the agricultural venture to help grubstake his future gold-hunting on a grander scale. When he lost almost his entire investment instead, he returned to North America.

The first-born son of a C.P.R. civil engineer living at Sangerville, Maine, Oakes had started his obsessive pursuit of gold in 1896 following his graduation with a liberal arts degree from Bowdoin College. After an unhappy stint selling for the Carter Ink Company, he was bitten by the Klondike madness then sweeping the U.S. and Canada.

He arrived in the Yukon during the spring of 1898 and almost immediately walked out to the less crowded but also promising gold finds of Alaska. With a Swedish partner, he soon discovered a gleaming quartz vein sprinkled with free-gold showings the size of peas in an inaccessible branch of the Kuskokwim River. He rounded up twenty miners to dig the bonanza but it turned out to be only a shallow pocket with narrow streaks of gold dust worth about six thousand dollars. The party floated out of the bush on a raft—the miners paid off and satisfied, the partners bankrupt. Their next venture was even less successful. They built a skiff to explore the Alaska coast, but were blown across the Bering Strait to Russia. They were captured by a band of Cossacks, escaped under rifle fire, and permanently abandoned Alaska.

For the next thirteen years Oakes roamed the world for gold, tapping likely-looking rocks in the Philippines, Australia, West Africa, the Belgian Congo, South Africa, Mexico and Death Valley, in California. Sometimes he scratched out enough gold to buy food, but more often he had to earn his grubstakes by farming, surveying or lumbering.

He arrived at Swastika in June, 1911. He was thirty-six, and still hunting. His total assets were a knapsack with prospecting tools and $2.65 in cash.

Some historians claim that the Timiskaming & Northern Ontario railroad conductor picked Oakes' destination by kicking him off the train at Swastika, because he couldn't pay the full fare to the Porcupine country. Others say that he got off the train voluntarily because he had heard about some unclaimed gold properties from a drunk in a Toronto Chinese restaurant. The prospectors who knew him insist that Oakes met a fellow sourdough on the train, and got off when he did to help kill a bottle of his companion's Scotch.

Oakes himself maintained that his trip was a scientific prospecting venture, based on government reports about the area and a conversation with Gilbert LaBine, at Haileybury. The latter backs up this version.

"On July 4, 1910, I met Oakes in a Haileybury hotel," LaBine recalls. "I remember the date, because it was the night of the Johnson-Jeffries fight. I told him about an area west of Swastika and advised him against going into the

Porcupine, which was by then entirely staked over. I went with him to buy a small grubstake, and next day accompanied him on the train as far as Swastika. There he disembarked and started prospecting."

Among the few prospectors who had not left Swastika for the Porcupine by the time Oakes arrived was Bill Wright, a Boer War veteran who had been a butcher in Lincolnshire before emigrating to Canada. His first job was painting the mill at the Mining Corporation of Canada property in Cobalt, then he began prospecting with Ed Hargreaves, his brother-in-law. They located their first ground on the fringe of the stakings east of Swastika near an unnamed lake, later called after Winnie Kirkland, a pretty clerk with the provincial Department of Lands & Forests. These claims eventually became the great Wright-Hargreaves Mines Limited, which started production in 1921 and has since paid out nearly $60 million in dividends. In 1936, with part of the income from his quarter share in the mine, Wright bought two Toronto papers, *The Mail & Empire* and *The Globe,* and merged them into *The Globe & Mail.* Hargreaves sold out his share in the property for three thousand dollars.

The Tough brothers—George, Tom, Rob and Jack—who held the contract for cutting a road from Swastika to Larder, had heard about the Wright-Hargreaves strike and decided to stake nearby. On the evening of January 6, 1912, they were outfitting themselves for the trek into the bush at Jimmy Doige's general store in Swastika when they met Oakes. He told them that some land originally staked by the Burrows brothers in 1907 was coming free later that night. The claims had been recorded, some trenches had been dug and a Cobalt bartender had even organized a syndicate to mine the properties, but the temptations of Porcupine had left them unworked for more than five years, throwing them open for restaking. Oakes could not profit from his knowledge, because he didn't have enough cash for the new recording fees. He offered to take the Toughs to the area in return for a partnership.

Eight inches of freshly fallen snow slowed the seven-mile walk to the abandoned diggings. Oakes guided the party through the drifts with a lantern, wearing five pairs of variously-patched trousers to ward off the bone-chilling fifty-five-below wind.

The Tough brothers and Oakes had just finished their restaking and were sipping tea when Bill Wright appeared, also eager to repossess the pits. He staked instead the adjoining western property. It was developed into the Sylvanite Gold Mine, whose five shafts eventually yielded gold ore worth more than $55 million.

Three days later George Tough pulled up a patch of moss under the snow and found a heavily mineralized vein. The ore was packed by canoe and portage to Swastika where assays showed average values of $457 a ton, with some chunks running as high as $700.

To get capital, the Toughs and Oakes had to bring in Clem Foster from Haileybury, a backer of some Cobalt mines. Foster sold the stock in England, but the deal ended in litigation. Many years later Oakes was awarded two hundred thousand dollars damages by the courts. He avenged himself on Foster by having the judgment reprinted and distributed throughout the mining industry.

By 1916, each month gold worth a hundred thousand dollars was being hauled by bucket out of the Tough–Oakes shaft. But the veins turned out to be narrow—a fault cut most of the gold off at three hundred feet. The shaft eventually was sunk to nineteen hundred feet, but values became so poor that the property was abandoned in 1928. It was dewatered and worked by Toburn Gold Mines Limited in 1931, but after another $3 million worth of gold had been extracted, the company gave up its charter.

Although Oakes had finally found the gold he had so long sought, he quickly realized that this was not the bonanza-sized discovery that could quiet his quest. He continued prospecting during the summer of 1912. One Wednesday afternoon in July, he spotted a spatter of gold on some rocks dipping into south Kirkland Lake. He staked two claims.

Wright immediately grabbed the two water lots next to Oakes, but in his hurry he overstaked one of the claims by seven acres.

Arthur Cockeram, another prospector, noticed the mistake and formed a syndicate to acquire the excess land. When Oakes incorporated his Lake Shore Mines Limited in 1914, he gave Wright two hundred thousand shares in the company for his two claims, and paid Cockeram and his partners thirty thousand dollars plus fifty thousand shares for their seven-acre triangle. Beneath this wedge rested two-thirds of Lake Shore's gold, including the richest ore ever found in Canada. Cockeram sold his stock at two dollars. Had he held it an extra few years, he would have become a millionaire.

Oakes himself had only thirty dollars in his pocket when he walked into Matheson to record his Lake Shore stake. He began with hand steels to dig into the little lakeside gold streak. Values were spotty but the mineralization persisted.

By the summer of 1913, Oakes' shaft was down a hundred feet. All the ore had been lugged up an inclined ladder in an old barrel. He had spent the little money he had received up to that time from the Tough–Oakes property and had tried to sell his fledgling mine to Charley Denison of Cobalt for eighty thousand dollars. But Denison, agreeing with the many engineers who had inspected the workings, declared them worthless. For the same reason Oakes was turned down by the mine-makers Noah Timmins and Jack Hammell, and by the castle-loving Toronto financier, Sir Henry Pellatt. Even Jimmy Doige, the Swastika merchant, preferred to give Oakes outright credit rather than trade Lake Shore notes for grub. Oakes' brother, a Maine lumber dealer, and his sister, a government stenographer in Washington, helped him to the limit of their funds.

"If Lake Shore," Oakes later complained, "had possessed as rich surface ore as the Tough–Oakes, I would never have had to go to the public for money." But for the few hundred feet of rock which then separated Oakes from the fabulously rich Lake Shore ore, he might have developed the only major gold mine in the world owned entirely by one man. Few Canadians outside the mining business realize how long the odds are of a mineral strike becoming a dividend-paying mine. Between 1904 and 1933, for instance, only 1.56 per cent of the mining companies incorporated in Ontario reached production.

Oakes finally decided in 1914 that his solo battle to make Lake Shore a mine was hopeless. He formed a company with 1,500,000 shares of one dollar par value and offered them for public subscription at forty cents. *The Globe* and *Saturday Night* refused to accept his ads. Lake Shore, they decided, smelled like a wildcat. Only *The Northern Miner* would run a small announcement. A few shares were sold but by 1917 Oakes was bankrupt again. He had spent $82,000 on development work; his immediate liabilities totalled $34,000.

With his last funds he rented a private railway car to bring into Kirkland a group of Buffalo business men. He bought them a roast beef dinner, poured their whisky strong, then offered them half a million treasury shares of Lake Shore at $32\frac{1}{2}$ cents. The beauty of the lake, gilded by the light of the harvest moon, did the rest. With the stub of a pencil, Oakes wrote out the sales agreement, dated August 6, 1917, on a piece of brown wrapping paper. The Buffalo financiers who held onto their shares eventually realized a return of one hundred and thirty times their investment in dividends alone.

Oakes used the newly acquired $150,000 to put up a primitive mill. It chugged along for a year with minimum results but its presence pushed the stock to 39 cents. A lateral cut that Oakes had run north from a drift under the lake in March, 1918, hit the north vein that turned out to be the district's main mineral break. It ran across the Lake Shore, sometimes a hundred feet wide, its values testing up to a spectacular $1,200 a ton. "Lake Shore had tougher sledding getting going than other mines," Oakes said, "because I had to cut through four hundred feet of hard porphy under the lake to get at the main vein. Once there, everything was all right." By the end of 1918, the little mill had turned out gold worth half a million dollars.

Every new stope that followed revealed more fully the magnificent anatomy of the Lake Shore deposit. The mine's production topped the output of the great Hollinger Consolidated in March of 1929. Lake Shore became the biggest producer in North America, and the sixth largest gold mine in the world.

The mine's dividend rate eventually reached 300 per cent a year—Oakes could have earned his staking fee in two minutes. The stock hit its peak of $62.50 in 1936. Oakes hired professionals to run the mine and spent most of the time during his visits to Kirkland Lake landscaping the property. He built a green-house to provide the miners with fresh vegetables, and in one winter grew seven tons of tomatoes.

To feed its hungry 2,500-ton-a-day mill, the Lake Shore's four shafts were extended continually farther into the earth. The No. 4 shaft reached 8,177 feet—the deepest gold-working horizon on the continent. Production had to be reduced in November 1939, owing to the many rock bursts at extreme depths.

The mine prospered without interruption during Oakes' lifetime, but by 1957 it was again in financial difficulties. Despite government subsidies of more than a hundred thousand dollars, profit for the first quarter of the year amounted to only $629. After having distributed dividends of more than $100 million, the company halted its payments in

1957. Control was acquired by George Boeckh, head of the Little Long Lac syndicate. He expanded Lake Shore's interests to western oil and gas (through Alminex Ltd. and Jerd Petroleums) and into the Arctic (through Le Moyne Ungava Mines Ltd.) Lake Shore now also owns its neighbour, the Wright-Hargreaves, and the Malartic Gold Fields in northwestern Quebec.

The men who worked with Oakes claimed that wealth changed his character only by accentuating its ugly streaks. The enormous drive and tough physical labour he had put into the creation of Lake Shore now lacked outlet. His fortune established, he lost all interest in mining, aside from the occasional investment. He took a trip around the world, then bought Buffalo utility magnate Walter Schoellkopf's mansion on the escarpment overlooking Niagara Falls. He renamed it Oak Hall and spent half a million dollars putting in a five-hole golf course, a swimming pool with underwater coloured lights, and an artificial hill built up by steam shovels to afford him a view in an otherwise flat country. (So that he would not tire of his panorama, Oakes had this hillock moved three times to different corners of his estate.)

The main door of Oak Hall was carved of black oak, four inches thick. The old-fashioned square knocker thudded through into the living-room—a tennis-court-sized hall sixty feet long and thirty feet wide. The entire downstairs was lined in English oak, including some of the original panels from Cardinal Wolsey's room at Hampton Court. Thirteenth-century columns enclosed a huge granite fireplace. The room's furniture was placed around a large table on which the treaty ending the Boxer Rebellion had been signed. Oakes also purchased the entire "Red Parlour" suite of the Queen's Hotel in Toronto where Sir John A. Macdonald had often sat with his Cabinet.

On a round-the-world cruise in 1922 Oakes met Eunice McIntyre, the daughter of an Australian civil servant. They were married that June. The bride was twenty-four; he was forty-eight. Back in Niagara Falls, Oakes began to remake the city on a grand scale. He charted a plan for moving all factories away from the river banks so that the shores could become parkland, and personally purchased the Ohio Brass plant across the street so that its smoke would not cloud his vision of the Falls. He gave the city land for the Oakes Garden Theatre and the Oakes Baseball Park, and built the Lady Oakes wing of the local hospital. His municipal gifts were generous, if not anonymous.

Oakes did not have the true instinct of philanthropy. He treated his gifts as investments. In 1937 he subscribed half a million dollars to the St. George's Hospital in London, an institution openly aided by the Royal Family. Two years later the King's honours list included a baronetcy for him.

His efforts in Canada to become a senator were equally costly, but less successful. He donated many hundreds of thousands of dollars to the Liberals for their 1930 campaign, and had already bought a large Rockcliffe mansion for his senatorial residence. But R. B. Bennett's Conservative victory squashed his political career.

Oakes complained at every opportunity that he paid more taxes on his personal income than any other Canadian. He estimated his 1933 tax assessment at three million dollars. One night in 1934, while travelling from his *château* at Kirkland to his mansion at Niagara, he decided to quit Canada for the tax-free West Indies. He resigned from the Lake Shore and never again set foot on Canadian soil. The 1935 annual report of the Lake Shore does not even mention his name. Oak Hall was later converted into a home for the chronically ill; its grounds are now a public park.

"This is what came to me that night I bid Canada good-bye," Oakes later told Gregory Clark of the *Toronto Star*. "If I died the succession duties would leave my family in the red, not the blue. True, I found the pot of gold at the end of the rainbow, and I found it in Canada. But I was paying out 80 per cent of the gold I'd found in taxes. Man don't work for that."

For his self-imposed exile in the Bahamas, Oakes bought from the American actress Maxine Elliott, for half a million dollars in cash, a twenty-bedroom pink-plaster house near Nassau on New Providence Island. He quickly became one of the island's most talked-about characters, sometimes parading around the estate in planter's white whipcord trousers and a beige sombrero, but turning up just as often among the island's road-building gangs in a dirty sweatshirt. He worked full shifts and was so convincing in his role that a compassionate American tourist once tipped him a shilling.

He directed successful raids on Palm Beach real estate, bought the 300-room British Colonial, Nassau's largest hotel, and spent half a million dollars redecorating it to match the colour of his wife's favourite sweater. (The hotel is still owned by his heirs, as are the Bahamas Country Club and seven thousand choice acres of real estate on New Providence.) Oakes' main gift to the island consisted of omnibuses for the natives. But instead of allowing them free rides, he established a charge of a penny for three miles.

Sir Harry was murdered sometime after midnight on July 8, 1943. He was sixty-eight. The killer had struck him brutally four times behind the left ear with a miner's hand pick, and had then burned insecticide over the body, concentrating the flame around the eyes. The corpse had been sprinkled with feathers dug out of the mattress. When it was discovered, they were still being blown gently over the mutilated body by the bedroom fan.

The only man accused of the murder at the time was Alfred de Marigny, the thirty-seven-year-old playboy who had married eighteen-year-old Nancy, Oakes' eldest daughter, a year before. His trial, which lasted twenty-two days and ended in acquittal, pushed much of the war news off the front pages. Speculation about the murderer is beyond the scope or intent of this book, but those who knew Oakes were not shocked by the news of his slaying, only by its timing. They wondered how Sir Harry with his legion of enemies had been able to survive so long.

Oakes' personal estate amounted to $14,686,000. A cache of gold bars rumoured to be his was found on nearby Eleuthera Island. The will divided all his money among the family. Nancy had her marriage to de Marigny annulled, opened a Nassau nightclub called The Hong Kong Room, married again and has since separated from her second husband, Ernst Lyssard von Hoyningen Huene, a German baron. Shirley, the other daughter, is a New York lawyer. One son is dead; the other two are in modest business positions.

Oakes' murder was not followed by the sugary editorials which customarily mark the death of wealthy Canadians. A few commented kindly about his perseverance in bringing the Lake Shore into production, but many resented his lack of gratitude to the country which had given him his wealth.

Shortly before his murder, one of the Lake Shore Mines' directors, who was visiting Nassau, asked Oakes: "Harry, what do you consider to have been your greatest error?"

"I made a mistake about that name," Oakes growled. "I should've called it Oakes Consolidated."

chapter 6

L I O N E L   F O R S Y T H

"We Canadians are a dull, unenterprising people.
We take time out from business for a cup of tea and a crumpet,
or to make love, or to have a snooze,
or to do any other damn thing that appeals to us at the time."

THE meal had been a good one. But now the audience of
New York bankers was becoming restless. Manicured fingers
nervously tapped after-dinner cigars as the guest was introduced. Once again, the financiers felt, they'd be forced to
fidget through a Canadian's lofty explanation of his country,
and how it differs from the United States.

The speaker was Lionel Avard Forsyth, B.A., M.A., D.C.L.,
LL.D., Q.C., president of the Dominion Steel & Coal Corporation. He appeared to be spilling out of his head-table
chair. He had insisted on two helpings of every course,
although his five-foot-five frame seemed already incapable

of supporting the more than two hundred pounds of his watermelon body. The preliminaries finished, he waddled up to the speaker's position.

"We Canadians are a dull, unenterprising people," Forsyth's gruff tones began vibrating out of his three chins. The bankers hitched themselves up a little. This fat Canadian had suddenly assumed the stance of a peremptory battleship captain.

"We have never enjoyed Prohibition, and never will," Forsyth rumbled on. "We Canadians take time out from business for a cup of tea and a crumpet, or to make love, or to have a snooze, or to do any other damn thing that appeals to us at the time."

Forsyth ended his twenty-seven-minute speech by reciting four verses of his own metaphysical poetry. The bankers, their cigars long cold and forgotten, clapped like first nighters at La Scala in Milan.

This kind of performance, repeated at least a dozen times a year, established Forsyth as a very rare bird indeed among the dull fowl that inhabit the presidential roosts of most Canadian corporations.

Forsyth made his way to one of Canada's top industrial positions by the sheer force of his energy, the honed brilliance of his intellectual equipment, and a vinegarish eloquence that made him a champion deflator of official stuffiness. The presidency of the Dominion Steel & Coal Corporation (better known as Dosco)—which he assumed in 1950, seven years before his death—was only the last of his many careers.

He had been a clipper-ship sailor, professional baseball player, railroad surveyor, streetcar driver, romance-languages professor, and Canada's highest-paid corporation lawyer. In 1946 he performed the unprecedented legal feat of arguing and winning three important cases before England's austere Privy Council. A particularly neat accomplishment, since he never attended law school. He was also an important breeder of Jersey cows, and paradoxically, a minor but accomplished poet.

Lionel Forsyth's presidency of the Dominion Steel & Coal Corporation places him as the last of the five men in this book who have been connected with the company. Lord Strathcona was a director of Dosco's two main predecessor firms for the twenty-three years before his death in 1914. Sir William Van Horne was vice-president of the Dominion Steel Corporation for two years and a director of the Dominion Coal Company from 1893 until 1917. Sir James Dunn was a young lawyer in Halifax, still studying at Dalhousie University, when he helped draw up the incorporation papers of the Dominion Iron & Steel Company, one of Dosco's antecedents. The man who formed the Dominion Steel & Coal Corporation from the welter of its promoter-milked predecessors was Sir Herbert Holt. He had been a director of the British Empire Steel Corporation since 1928, and he remained a Dosco director until his death in 1941.

Forsyth was never stuffy in his handling of Dosco affairs. His good friends called him "Laddie". To a few close pals he was "Bunny". Deep crow's feet ran from the corners of his eyes, suggesting the glimmer of a constant smile, barely under control. Even at sixty-seven—his age when he died—he had the energy of half his years.

But his dimensions did require some special precautions. Forsyth had zippers on the sides of his vests, which he could open while sitting. Zipped up, the vests helped prop up his errant waistline. This arrangement was labelled "the Forsyth Sagger" by Murray Chipman, a Montreal executive who was often his luncheon companion. Trans-Canada Air Lines managed to keep him comfortable by clamping extra-length safety belts to his airplane seat. Standard equipment wouldn't reach round him.

Forsyth's speeches reflected his personal versatility. He preferred business topics, but also talked on medical history, higher mathematics, Canadian literature, philosophy, the Song of Solomon, small-town living, and the strange career of D. A. Lafortune, the marathon orator, elected to the Canadian House of Commons in 1911, who filled thirty pages of Hansard at a time.

Forsyth wrote his speeches out on long sheets of bond paper in pencil, using a sermon-like development of his theme. Although his talks bristled with rough wit, he despised the standard after-dinner speaker's gambit of being reminded of a story.

"This type of speaker," he once told a friend, "far from being reminded of a story, has been in a state of continuous agony for fear he will forget it." Forsyth's audiences were seldom bored. But at a Halifax luncheon on a steaming Friday afternoon in July, 1955, he realized that he was talking to a roomful of dozers. He shocked his audience into frightened wakefulness by suddenly chanting in a loud, nasal singsong :

> "Who put the benzedrine
> In Mrs. Murphy's Ovaltine?"

In a typical Forsyth anecdote, a bejewelled, befurred lady, leading a crew-cut poodle on a blue ribbon, walks into a psychiatrist's office, noisily demanding attention. "Madam, do be seated. I'm sure I can help," says the doctor. "Tell me what is the matter with you?" The distraught matron replies at once : "There's nothing the matter with me, doctor. It's my husband here. He thinks he's a dog."

To demonstrate the weakness of basing all judgements on statistics, Forsyth told the story of the lumber camp in Northern Quebec, staffed by fifty lumberjacks and two women cooks. When one of the loggers seduced one of the cooks, the statistics showed that 50 per cent of the women had been seduced by 2 per cent of the men.

He was most serious when addressing groups of Dosco employees. "The seed of our toil," he would thunder at them, "watered with the sweat of our brows, has now ripened into the fruits of our labours." Nearly all of Forsyth's speeches ended in rhymed imagery—verses from one of a dozen poems whose author he never identified. When pressed, he would admit that they were written by "a Canadian poet of the Upper St. Lawrence School". Only a few close friends knew that these fragments were the sole glimpses Forsyth ever allowed the public of his own poetry. He composed verses almost continually for forty years, but never passed a poem for publication. He once wrote this autobiographical verse describing his mood of ambitious restlessness :

"It is the seas I have not sailed
That beat against my breast,
It is the heights I have not scaled
That will not let me rest,
It is the paths I have not gone
That tempt my restless feet,
It is the flowers I have not known
That are forever sweet,
It is the lips I have not kissed
That lure my soul astray,
It is the voice my soul has missed
That calls me night and day."

When he found time, Forsyth worked on a book about Thomas Gray, his favourite poet. It was never finished. He was serious about his hobbies but found little time for them. He enjoyed shooting ducks among the reed beds of Lake St. Francis, described himself as an ardent but indifferent golfer. At his Folleigh Farm in Dundee, Que., he tried to improve the strain of Canadian Jerseys. On week-ends he drove his dinted station wagon to the nearby Ormstown Fair, where his stock won many prizes.

He entertained most business friends in his Montreal residence, the least pretentious of the mansions lining Westmount's fashionable Sunnyside Drive. Invitations to his annual Christmas parties were in his typically free-handed style of doggerel :

> "Beneath the mistletoe to trade a kiss,
> And quaff a cup of eggnog Christmas day—
> If you can take out time enough for this,
> Drop in and see us when you pass this way."

Forsyth used even wilder rhymes in his private family mail. On August 18, 1955 he called in his secretary and dictated a hunting-trip invitation to his brother John, then personnel manager of the New York Telephone Company :

> "Twenty-fourth day of September
> Is the date you must remember
> And the answer must be yea, not nay.
> Ere the sun announces dawn,
> We must rise, get fed, be gone.
> Oh can you make it brother?
> Whadda ya say?"

Brother John's reply seemed to threaten the Dosco president's claim on the Forsyth clan poet laureateship.

> "Ye needna make an awfu' fuss
> Aboot yer bran' new blunderbuss
> I thought that ye should hae it just
> Tae aid yer shootin'.
> I'll be there the night before
> Tae view wi' bleary eyes and sore
> Dawn on September twenty-four
> Ye'll no be dootin' !"

Forsyth belonged to eleven clubs, but preferred his happy home life, especially the visits of his daughter and son who had settled in Halifax. This continued personal link fitted in well with his intense feelings toward Nova Scotia. "My cup of pride would have been filled to overflowing," he often told Eastern audiences in mock seriousness, "if I could have uttered my first feeble cry on the island of Cape Breton. But one can't have everything."

His first distinguishable word was the Spanish *muchacho,* in imitation of his father calling for the native boy at Iloilo, in the Philippines. Forsyth spent most of his pre-school years sailing round the world on his father's *Harvest Queen,* a two-thousand-ton square rigger. "I cut my teeth on a marlin spike, and I could box the compass before I could recite the alphabet," he boasted.

Young Lionel entered Grade Two of the Windsor Academy in 1897 and by the end of the year was promoted to Grade Three—although school records show him attending only $61\frac{1}{2}$ days. That was the year he met an eight-year-old fellow pupil, Elsie Maie Dimock, whom he married eighteen years later.

He graduated in Arts from the University of King's College at Windsor, N.S., in 1909, after playing fullback on the university football squad and goalie for the Windsor team in the Nova Scotia Hockey League. He spent one summer as second baseman on a professional Maritime baseball team. He also worked as a timekeeper on wharf construction in western Nova Scotia and was rod man on a survey team in northern New Brunswick during construction of the National Transcontinental Railway.

For a short time after graduation, Forsyth thought of entering a Church of England seminary. "But," he said later, "it didn't take me long to get over that." Instead he went to Harvard University for a graduate course in the origins of the French and German languages. He worked his way through this highbrow curriculum by driving a street-car for the Boston Railway Company. He was then appointed Associate Professor of Romance Languages at Trinity College, in Durham, North Carolina, now Duke University.

When Forsyth returned to Canada in 1913 and couldn't find any academic openings, he joined the Bank of Nova Scotia as Chief Accountant's Clerk, in Toronto. One of his duties was to operate the bank's cafeteria. He hated getting up early and made a deal with a waiter from Bowles Lunch, next door, to sneak him a breakfast tray into the lunch-room at nine o'clock. One day he was caught enjoying his leisurely breakfast and banished to the bank's branch in Havana. During his eighteen months in Cuba he learned Spanish and enough about banking to realize he wasn't meant to be a banker.

Forsyth returned to the academic life in 1915 as a modern-languages professor at the University of King's College. While he was at King's, W. M. Christie, the Hants County prosecutor, interested him in the legal profession and he began teaching himself law after classes. In 1918 Forsyth was admitted to the Nova Scotia bar, and in six months he was arguing everything from collections to divorce cases.

One of his first important trials was a fierce court battle against the Dominion Coal Company, part of the corporation he later headed. He successfully represented striking miners and won an injunction against a pay cut planned by management. Later he won a case against Halifax Shipyards Limited (another Dosco subsidiary) when he established that the company had no right to prevent picketing.

By 1926, thirty-six-year-old Forsyth had a booming practice, earning him thirty thousand dollars a year, but he was becoming restless with the limited opportunities of the Maritimes. When he was asked to join Montgomery, McMichael, Common, Howard & Ker in Montreal, Canada's largest law firm, he decided to move, despite the new burden of having to learn Quebec's vastly different legal code. On his way from Halifax, he stayed up all night with a nine-hundred-page book on the Napoleonic Code; and next day, when he was orally examined by a partner in the firm, he not only passed, but witnesses claim he cross-examined his questioner.

Forsyth stayed with the Montreal legal firm for twenty-three years, developing Canada's most varied and most lucrative law practice. He defended clients in tax, labour, combines, corporation, and admiralty law cases. Some of his combines and labour trial addresses are still used as textbook examples of brilliant legal procedure. His law practice grew so spectacularly that to satisfy the cross-country demands of his clients, he was forced to take the bar exams of five provinces. He eventually became a director of forty-six companies.

Forsyth spent most of his time handling one of his firm's largest clients—the affairs of the Dominion Steel & Coal Corporation—and from 1928 he acted as Dosco's general counsel. More than the Company's importance to his native Nova Scotia attracted Forsyth to the Dosco account. Unravelling the steel and coal company's then debt-ridden finances was the kind of challenge he enjoyed.

The digging of coal began in the Maritimes in 1720, when the French soldiers tried to keep warm while building the fortress of Louisbourg, which was supposed to maintain the sovereignty of France forever over North America. Dosco's corporate roots stretched back to before Confederation. In 1824, England's George IV granted his brother the Duke of York a lease to all of Nova Scotia's minerals, but the spendthrift Duke assigned the right to his creditors—mostly jewellers—who formed the General Mining Association to exploit Cape Breton's coal. In 1872, two Scotsmen built a four-thousand-dollar forging plant at New Glasgow called the Hope Iron Works to make fastenings for sailing ships. In 1899, the successor companies of these pioneering ventures joined their assets to become "Disco" (Dominion Iron & Steel Co.), beginning the game of Scrabble which sums up the company's history.

"Disco" became "Besco" (British Empire Steel Corp.) in 1920, following another painfully negotiated merger. But capitalization far greater than warranted by the earning power of the merged properties eventually forced a new set of initials. Between 1928 and 1930 Forsyth helped negotiate the final change. "Besco" became "Dosco", with assets carried on the former company's balance sheets at $160 millions, written down to $53 millions. Dosco was then such a poor financial risk that for a $5 million loan negotiated in 1933,

Canadian banks demanded collateral worth $7.5 million. In 1935 Nova Scotia Premier G. S. Harrington called Dosco stock "pure, unadulterated water."

Forsyth's legal approach to the entangled problems of the corporation had so impressed successive Dosco managements that in 1949 the board of directors unanimously voted him the presidency. The appointment was reflected in a tangible salute to his abilities from the hard-headed Bay Street stock traders. On December 19, 1949, the day he moved into his green-carpeted downtown Montreal presidential office, Dosco shares jumped from $17.50 to $19.00—the biggest increase in three years.*

Forsyth jokingly described his function at Dosco in the French *le bon père de famille,* which he freely translated as "everybody works but Father." While he did delegate authority, arguments were settled with his "We'll take my version of it."

The Dosco herd of companies comprises Canada's most important coal mines, the world's largest submarine iron-ore reserves, a 543-acre steel mill at Sydney with one-fifth of the country's primary steel-making capacity, seventeen fabricating plants, three railroads, and three shipping lines. The coal mines arch out to sea from an elliptical thirty-five-mile shore frontage around Sydney, dipping up to six miles under the Atlantic. Miners spend two hours a day riding to and from the workings along ninety-two miles of submarine railroad. The iron-ore diggings are attached to Bell Island, thirteen

* In October 1957, control of the company was acquired by A. V. Roe Canada Limited, part of the Hawker Siddeley Group Limited, of London, England.

square miles of rock humping out of Conception Bay, off Newfoundland's east coast. The miners toil at rock faces beneath salt water twenty fathoms deep.

Forsyth spectacularly reactivated this fossilized giant, marching Dosco's net income from $12 million to $20 million in the brief seven years he was its chief. He insisted that he had only one formula for success. "I am willing," he chuckled, "to allow other people to tell me what they know."

A few weeks after he became president, Forsyth launched a hundred-million-dollar campaign to remake the company. He proudly flapped his stubby arms at a group of his Sydney steel-workers, and shouted : "We're flying now, boys!"

Forsyth refused to follow the attitude of his Dosco predecessors by dealing with labour problems in terms of a master-servant relationship. "The conflict of basic ideology between management and labour has outlived its usefulness," he flatly asserted.

Dosco once had and deserved Canada's worst labour record. "Learn to hate the company with all the honesty in your hearts!" the union magazine urged in 1925. The coal miners had demanded a 10 per cent raise, the company answered with a proposal to cut pay by 10 per cent. On March 2 the company abruptly stopped issuing credit at its stores, where employees had previously been urged to buy all their food, clothing and furniture. Four days later twelve hundred miners laid down their picks to begin one of the bloodiest strikes in Canadian labour history. In June the gradually starving miners looted Glace Bay company stores. Troops were brought in from Halifax and Toronto. In the clashes that followed forty miners were injured and one, William Davis, was killed. The anniversary of his death is still observed as a contract holiday at Dosco pits.

Against this envenomed background, Forsyth enforced his enlightened labour policies with almost religious fervour. He would not allow his managers to speak roughly to trade-union officers, and directed that labour wage-increase requests should not be referred to as "demands", but as "proposals."

Forsyth's rough humour salvaged some potentially explosive labour situations. Soon after he took over the presidency he walked into a tension-charged union-management meeting. Sensing the hate and suspicion in the room, he drew back his coat sleeves and told the suddenly relaxed gathering: "Look boys, there's nothing up my sleeves but my elbows."

The windy afternoon of March 10, 1953, when his wife officially opened the new Sydney blooming mill, was Forsyth's proudest moment at Dosco. Just before Mrs. Forsyth pulled the lever that sent the first seven-ton ingot ripping through the shiny rollers of the new mill, Ben O'Neill, president of Dosco's United Steel Workers local, interrupted her and apologized to Forsyth for "soliciting new members on company time", then presented his wife with an honorary union membership card.

It was the dramatic pay-off to Forsyth's labour crusade, but his humour was not dulled by sentiment. "This," he said, "may run into domestic complications. She may call on the union for support if she feels she is under-paid. It may be a question for negotiations."

Forsyth also helped boost morale by spending more time underground than all previous Dosco presidents put together.

His miner's belt buckled to its first notch, he would crawl through the most inaccessible coal and iron-ore drifts to chat with his "boys"—men never quite the same after they'd been startled by the sudden apparition of their tubby boss, six miles under the Atlantic.

To push lagging steel production, Forsyth took six weeks away from his president's desk in 1954 and became a travelling salesman. He went to Europe and came back with orders worth a hundred million dollars, one of the largest export transactions in Canadian business history. He modernized coal-mining operations by introducing machines capable of clawing out of the earth in two minutes enough coal to heat the average house for a full winter.

As part of his effort to wake up the dormant coal market, Forsyth set up a separate department in a low-ceilinged shack at Glace Bay, charged with designing a furnace that would eliminate the messiness and inconvenience of coal heating. Without its white enamel cover, the resultant down-draught, air-pressure home-heating unit looked like a Rube Goldberg version of a whiskey still. To help the gadget's sales, Forsyth made a speaking tour of the Maritimes. "Get behind the industry and see to it that every Nova Scotian gets right with himself and uses Nova Scotia coal, the thrifty fuel, if you know what's good for you!" he thundered at his audiences.

During the private head-table chatter after his speeches, someone would inevitably ask Forsyth why, at fifty-nine, he had decided to give up the country's best law practice to take on the unrewarding task of bossing Canada's least prosperous steel company.

Forsyth gave a romantic explanation. "To some," he would say, "the steel-and-coal industry may seem to have a complete absence of the lure of the unknown. But for me, thank God, it's different. Something I've not yet seen, heard or experienced awaits me around every corner."

Shortly before his death on January 1, 1957, from leukemia, he sat in Montreal's Saint James's Club, reminiscing with a close friend about the fullness of his life. "I've had many different occupations," he said. "But I never did anything from which I didn't get sixty minutes of pleasure for every hour of work."

chapter 7

GILBERT LaBINE

"You never can tell,
my next visitor might be Saint Joseph."

MOST of the primitive sourdoughs who roamed the rolling rock desert of the Precambrian Shield, staking the claims that launched Canadian mining as a major industry, have already become faceless, almost legendary characters of an only half-remembered era. Such crusty bush tramps as Benny Hollinger and Sandy McIntyre have been replaced by a new generation of mine makers—men more familiar with the promoter's telephone than the prospector's sampling pick.

The only Canadian who has bridged these styles in mine making with spectacular success is Gilbert LaBine, the adventurous bushwhacker who pushed Canada into the atomic age a quarter of a century ago, and is still numbered among the most influential mining men on Toronto's Bay Street.

LaBine's current fortune is concentrated in Gunnar Mines —Canada's first dividend-paying uranium producer and his fourth major uranium strike—now exploiting a mammoth, sausage-shaped deposit near Lake Athabaska, in northern Saskatchewan. With the forcefulness that has characterized his career, seventy-year-old LaBine proclaims : "I've produced a lot of uranium, and I'll produce a hell of a lot more."

Nearly thirty years ago, on the unseasonably cold morning of May 16, 1930, at a forlorn inlet off Great Bear Lake less than a day's walk from the Arctic Circle, LaBine chopped a plum-sized blob out of a virgin crag sloping into the bay's still-frozen water.

It turned out to be the most significant mineral strike in Canadian history—the first commercial showing found in this country of pitchblende, the mother ore of radium and uranium.

LaBine's discovery eventually trebled the world's radium supply, shattering the Belgian monopoly over its curative rays. Ultimately, it was this deposit's uranium that provided the wrath for the bomb that ended World War II. "If it had not been for the vision and determination of Gilbert LaBine, we wouldn't have had the bomb in time," wrote Dr. William L. Laurence, the science editor of *The New York Times*, who witnessed the carnage of Nagasaki.

LaBine stopped prospecting ten years ago, but his spare 180-pound, six-foot frame gives the impression that he can still hike a canoe through the bush without strain. His varnish-pale face has been abraded by the Arctic winds of its once healthy tint. The whites of his blue eyes have been left permanently bloodshot by repeated snow blindness. He talks in a low-pitched growl, with a dogged but curiously impersonal fluency that shuts the casual visitor completely out of the man's inner mind. He can evade some topics with a dexterous courtesy that suggests much practice.

LaBine's career has not followed the classic pattern of the successful prospector whose pilgrimages into the bush were rewarded with one of those quick strikes of accidental good fortune that have been so influential in Canadian mining history. His discovery of Eldorado was no accident. It represented a climax for which he had been rehearsing during a lifetime spent tramping through the geologically unknown northern belts of Canada traversed previously only by this country's first explorers and the fur trappers who followed.

"Gilbert LaBine," *The Northern Miner* once editorialized "has been called a man of destiny—so he is, but it is a destiny of his own making." The basis of this self-determinism is the fact that at the time LaBine made the Great Bear Lake discovery, he had already been seeking pitchblende in Canada for more than a decade. He was one of the very few sourdoughs in the world who could identify the rare mineral, never before found in the western hemisphere. "Not one other prospector in a thousand would have recognized it," says John W. Carrington, editor of *The Northern Miner*. "Even if he had, he certainly wouldn't have staked a claim twelve hundred miles from the nearest railroad, as LaBine did."

LaBine's strike, spectacular as it was, turned out to have been the simpler achievement, compared with his battle to bring the mine into production. Most prospectors would have sold their claims to a syndicate, blown the money on a spree, then set off to search again. But LaBine managed to turn his discovery into an operating property, and after he lost it through government expropriation during World War II, he promptly found and financed two more uranium producers.

Unlike other prospectors who have risen to corporate command, LaBine doesn't dismiss administrative work as suitable only for less imaginative heads. "Nothing of importance comes to this office without getting to his desk," says Joseph LaBine, Gilbert's eldest son and a Gunnar vice-president.

LaBine is seldom bored by office routine, but the weeks before his frequent trips into the bush are unbearable for his staff. He stomps around, impatiently fussing over details usually ignored. He often talks about another long prospecting trek, but usually limits his excursions to walks around the Gunnar property. Few of his miners recognize him.

Dressed as he is in beautifully tailored dark suits and subdued ties, his appearance gives little support to the tales of his stamina in Arctic blizzards. He hates publicity. In 1949 Leonard Haynes, the Hollywood producer, tried to persuade him to have his life story filmed. "I put the can on that one," says LaBine. The honours he prizes most are the Curie medal he won in 1938, and his appointment, two years later, to the University of Toronto board of governors.

Away from the office LaBine hunts, curls and plays golf, but these are diversions, not passions. His favourite reading is the journals he has collected of early Canadian explorers. He spends one winter month in Florida, and four weeks at his summer cottage on Georgian Bay. Although he is a grand-father a dozen times over, at family water-polo contests LaBine can still move faster than those half his age. In 1954 he sold his 300-acre farm at Maple, Ontario, and moved into a fifteen-room house in Toronto's Bayview district.

With the bristling Irish pride he has inherited from his parents, LaBine insists that he regards his independence from bosses as his main accomplishment. "I've worked less than a year for any other man," he boasts.

His only employer was the old University Mine, where he laboured briefly as a miner during the Cobalt rush, which lured him away at sixteen from his father's farm at West-meath, Ont. A year later, in 1907, LaBine quit to become a prospector and almost immediately staked some silver-bear-ing claims east of Cobalt. He sold out for five thousand dollars.

That winter LaBine attended a short course at the Hailey-bury School of Mines being given by Dr. W. G. Miller, the provincial geologist. Most of Miller's class was anxious only to learn the short cuts of gold and silver prospecting, but LaBine was intrigued with Miller's theory that there might be radium-bearing pitchblende in the Cobalt area. Marie Curie had just been awarded her second Nobel Prize for isolating metallic radium. She had used ore from Joachims-thal, near Karlsbad in Czechoslovakia, which occurred in rock structures remarkably like the Cobalt formations. Miller showed LaBine samples of pitchblende and taught him to identify it through the element's remarkably heavy specific gravity.

LaBine then began to range northward, scouring the bush for mineral showings worth a mine. His diet was the yield of his fishing rod and a 30/30 Winchester, supplemented by the crude bread he baked over camp-fires. "The bush," he says, leaning heavily into the red-leather upholstery of his executive chair, "is good to any God-fearing man with a rifle and a pinch of salt."

During one prospecting trip along the Eastmain River, east of James Bay, in 1912, LaBine collected his samples by lugging a supply-heavy canoe over muskeg so spongy that he had to strap on snowshoes to keep from sinking out of sight.

He was resting between prospecting trips in Toronto during the fall of 1916, when he overheard two prospectors talking about a radioactive hill near Perth, Ontario. He jumped into a taxi and drove two hundred miles to investigate the rumour. It was a false lead. A year later, he found some lightly radioactive rocks in Haliburton County, in central Ontario.

Despite such flurries of pitchblende fever, LaBine concentrated on the search for more common minerals. His best strike occurred during a 1917 trip into the Rice Lake area of southeastern Manitoba.

After weeks of rock chipping with indifferent results, he woke up at 4 A.M. one day, washed his face in a nearby creek, and on his way back through the mist-shrouded forest, found free gold in twenty-five places. He ran into camp, shouting to his partner, "My God, this is an Eldorado!"

A company called Eldorado Gold Mines Limited was organized, with LaBine as managing director. Half a million dollars raised through stock sales was used in 1927 for six thousand feet of underground exploration. The encouraging surface showings turned out to be thin veins that pinched out at 525 feet. Rather than drain the funds remaining in the treasury on further drilling, LaBine resolved to find his company another mine.

It was a time of intense gold-prospecting activity. Dozens of rushes confirmed the dimensions of wealth under the scented muskeg of northern Ontario and Quebec. The frenzied manoeuvres of the stock speculators drove prospectors ever deeper into the sub-Arctic.

Rumours of copper and gold showings interested LaBine in the slab of wilderness between the Coppermine River and Great Bear Lake—a vast no man's land dividing the territory of the Eskimos and the hunting ground of their ancestral enemies, the Indians. The region had remained inviolate, because a thousand-mile lacework of rock-and-lake strewn swamp separated it from Edmonton, the nearest city. For more than a century explorers had returned with tales of mineral riches. Samuel Hearne, the Hudson's Bay Company trader who set out in 1770 to find the copper mines legendary with the Chippewa Indians, reported the use of copper tools, but could find only scatterings of the mineral.

A trapper named Charles Sloane, during a 1922 expedition into the area, had brought out chunks of copper—at that time not considered worth mining so far from transportation facilities. But by 1929 copper had risen to twenty-four cents a pound. LaBine decided to visit the area. He hired Leigh

Britnell of Winnipeg (at $1.75 an air mile) to fly him into Hunter Bay, near the north-east tip of Great Bear Lake, making arrangements to be picked up three weeks later. Prospecting by air was then still considered a risky innovation.

A few days after LaBine's arrival, the trapper Sloane walked out of the bush. He was baffled at how LaBine had beaten him to the copper find. "I slid in on a moonbeam," LaBine jokingly explained. Later he staked four claims with rich copper and bismuth showings. He also found some gold ore assaying about twenty dollars a ton. But his samples later proved that extraction would be unprofitable, due to the deposit's isolation.

Sloan soon left to trek his way over his trap route back to civilization, while LaBine waited for his pick-up plane. Bad flying weather delayed its landing and he had to keep himself alive by fishing and hunting. But the many fly bites almost immobilized him. "I looked like a raw piece of liver," he recalls. During a break between storms an aircraft landed, piloted by C. H. "Punch" Dickins, one of Canada's best-known pioneer bush pilots.

Thirty miles south of Hunter Bay, along the shore of McTavish Arm, LaBine, peering through the humming shrouds of the biplane, noticed some rocks with smudges of peach red barely visible against the lowering rays of the afternoon sun. This was an indication of cobalt bloom, and LaBine knew that where there was cobalt, there might be silver, and possibly pitchblende. "I suddenly realized," he said later, "that I was in elephant country."

LaBine jabbed Dickins in the ribs, yelling at him to drop

and circle the area. "We were flying along the east shore of the lake," Dickins remembers, "when LaBine started to jump around and make sketches in his field book. He asked me if I thought I could find the spot again."

During the winter of 1929, LaBine searched the Department of the Interior archives in Ottawa and found a report by Dr. J. Mackintosh Bell, who had toured Great Bear Lake for the Geological Survey of Canada in 1900. Bell had noticed the cobalt bloom, which LaBine saw from the air, at an inlet he named Echo Bay. "The colours," Bell reported, "gave scintillating reflections in deep, transparent water, which suggested a locality to lure the prospector."

Next spring, after arranging for his brother Charles to lead a supply party down the Mackenzie River, LaBine flew from Fort McMurray, Alberta, to the headwaters of the Camsell River, intending to explore the unknown region between his landing spot and Echo Bay. His partner was Charles E. St. Paul, one of the original stakers near the Howey Gold Mine and an occasional prospecting companion of LaBine's since 1913.

To haul their sixteen hundred pounds of supplies—including a sectional canoe—the two men made a crude sleigh. They boosted their weakening pulling power by hoisting a sail. For six weeks they marched thirty miles a day in forty-below winds, taking samples from the rocks along the way. They saw only the occasional caribou, heard nothing but the lonely chatter of the Arctic pine squirrel.

Their boots slipped on the lake ice. To gain traction they tied hacksaw blades to their frozen soles. Unaccustomed to the dazzling spring sun on the burnished ice, St. Paul was blinded. He could still help pull the sleigh, but he had to be guided like a blinkered ox.

In the evening of May 14, they staggered into Echo Bay. St. Paul's eyes were sightless pits of pain. LaBine set up camp and began to poultice his partner's face with tea leaves dipped in melted snow.

At ten o'clock on the morning of May 16, LaBine left St. Paul for a scouting trip across the frozen bay. In less than an hour he found a treeless jut of shoreline shining with splashes of cobalt bloom.

"I noticed a great wall," LaBine recalls. "It had a strip of dark, greenish-black, lava-like substance zigzagging through it. Near the water it widened into a three-inch vein. Following it along, I found a piece of ore probably the size of a plum. I chipped it off with my hammer. It was solid pitchblende. I knew it, because I felt its specific gravity. You couldn't mistake it."

During the next three hours, LaBine discovered copper ore so pure that he carved his initials in it. (They're still there.) He also traced ten-foot-wide layers of silver ore, winding across the rock like a highway. He immediately staked two claims to cover the mineralized section, now known as LaBine Point. LaBine was so excited about the pitchblende that he forgot to tell St. Paul of the accompanying silver. They stayed at Echo Bay until St. Paul could travel again, then hurried off to Hunter Bay, thirty miles due north, to meet their supply party.

Hunter Bay was no longer the quiet inlet LaBine had visited the previous summer. The stories of its copper and gold deposits had attracted dozens of prospectors—and some were gradually drifting south, towards his pitchblende strike. LaBine rushed back to Echo Bay as soon as his brother arrived with their heavy equipment. As he ran eagerly up from shore, he incredulously caught the tangy smell of frying bacon. Directly over his momentous discovery sat three prospectors, cooking their supper. LaBine's nervous small talk soon established that the group, belonging to Dominion Explorers Limited, was interested in the gold possibilities of the rock-ribbed ridges farther south along Great Bear's shore. They were unschooled sourdoughs, trained only in spotting the quartz formations that favour gold. "If they had assayed their boots," says LaBine, "they would have found Eldorado."

That season LaBine's crew staked the shore around the original find, bagged a few samples, and on September 9 flew out to Fort McMurray. "We have secured holdings in what looks like the biggest mining camp ever discovered in Canada," LaBine optimistically informed the stockholders of Eldorado Gold Mines. He was voted a million and a half shares out of the company's funds for his discovery.

During the winter, news of the radium find so stirred the Depression-dampened spirits of treasure seekers all over the world that in the spring of 1931 every available bush plane in Canada was hired for a shuttle service into Great Bear Lake. A group of Germans arrived in the July heat, dressed for Arctic blizzards. The stakers included a Russian prince with his princess and bearded valet, and an Arab sheik who wandered aimlessly along the shore of the lake, his robes catching in the stunted conifers.

Tom Creighton, a skilled woodsman who had earlier helped stake the great Flin Flon Mine in northern Manitoba, used the most original technique for locating radium traces. He dropped undeveloped films on likely looking rocks; radioactivity showed up on the negative as streaks of light. Nearly five thousand claims were staked that year but the only mine that has ever produced in the region is Eldorado.

As soon as the ice broke up in the summer of 1932, LaBine shipped out twenty tons of semi-refined ore to metallurgical labs in Ottawa. Dr. G. S. Whitby, director of the National Research Council's Chemistry Division, reported that Echo Bay ore was a "chemical museum," containing not only pitchblende in larger quantities than any rock then known in the world, but fifty-three other minerals as well, including silver, copper, lead, zinc, cobalt, iron, and large amounts of uranium.

To gain initial capital for his mine, LaBine blasted out the surface silver—some of it running to a fantastic twenty thousand ounces per ton. Six hundred bags of unrefined silver, worth a million dollars, were stacked in the cockpits of flimsy bush planes and flown out to Fort Rae. Then river steamers chugged the ore upstream to the Northern Alberta Railways terminal at Waterways.

A year-round camp of tar shacks soon clustered near the Echo Bay workings. LaBine applied to the Government for permission to call his settlement Radium City, but the authorities rejected the title as too grandiose. They named the huddle of huts Port Radium. Twenty-five hard-rock miners were meanwhile sinking a shaft through the permafrost. Every pound of food and equipment had to be flown in by the brittle bush planes, buzzing northward like swarming bees. At a charge of $1.50 a pound for air-freight, a bottle of Port Radium whisky cost $11.50.

Despite its proven value, Canadian investors remained skeptical about the possibility of bringing out Eldorado's ore economically. Great Bear Lake's navigation season lasts only two months and its only link with the Mackenzie system is the shallow Great Bear River, broken by an eight-mile jag of cataracts. The fifteen-hundred-mile trip up the Mac-Kenzie is obstructed by impassable rapids between Fort Smith and Fort Fitzgerald. At first, LaBine loaded his ore on Hudson's Bay Company boats at Fort Norman. But after a freight-rate fight, he built his own ships.

By 1933 LaBine had raised enough development money from U.S. investors to put up a radium refinery at Port Hope, Ontario, sixty miles east of Toronto, near some cheap sources of the acid necessary for the process. Milling could not be done at the mine, because seven tons of chemicals were required to treat a ton of pitchblende. It took from late in 1933 to November 16, 1937, to produce the first ounce of radium —a pinch of white powder the size of a kitchen match.

Until the 1912 discovery of pitchblende at the Katanga copper mine, in an inaccessible jungle clearing of the Belgian Congo, the world supply of radium was limited to a few grams a year, grudgingly yielded by diggings at Joach-imsthal, in Czechoslovakia. The year that LaBine made his discovery the world supply of radium amounted to just over half a pound, worth twenty-two million dollars. LaBine's strike trebled the mineral's stocks, slashing the Belgian $70,000 per gram price to $20,000. "We fought the Belgian cartel in every capital of the world," says LaBine. "By 1939, we were pushing them around and selling nearly half the world's radium."

Uranium, one of the Port Hope refinery's byproducts, was causing LaBine considerable difficulties. Although uranium was first isolated by the German chemist Martin Klaproth in 1789, its market in the thirties was limited to a few tons a year for colouring pottery. LaBine stored the excess uranium in farmers' silos and specially built bins surrounding the plant. When these were filled up, it was piled on the company's wharves and later loaded on barges and dumped into Lake Ontario.

LaBine believed—with the foresight that marked his career as a prospector—that the uranium would some day become a valuable asset. "Research has been most active with uranium," he told his 1939 meeting of shareholders. "Much work is being done on the development of energy through its fission." Scientists had confided to LaBine that uranium contained U235, a material capable of releasing unlimited energy. The difficulty was that because of uranium's low U235 content (0.7%), they estimated it would take a thousand years to make an ounce of U235.

LaBine sent uranium samples to hundreds of British and American scientists following a 1940 conversation with an English Nobel Prize winner in chemistry, then engaged in nuclear research. "I asked him how big his work might be," says LaBine. "He told me that it could be the most important discovery in the civilized world since the birth of Christ."

The outbreak of World War II ruined LaBine's radium business, because the countries that had been his largest customers were invaded by the Nazis. In June 1940 he ordered the pump compressors stopped, and his mine closed. The now unrestrained frigid water of Great Bear seeped back into the workings.

Although Eldorado's financial statements showed a comfortable assets-to-liabilities ratio, the banks refused to accept the piles of ore at Port Hope as loan collateral. To keep his company alive, LaBine pledged personal securities worth a million dollars. With his income and his occupation cut off by war, LaBine paced his office, worrying about his future. Then, just after lunch on April 21, 1942, LaBine got an urgent call from C. D. Howe, the Minister of Munitions and Supply, to come to Ottawa that night. Howe ordered LaBine to reopen his mine at crash speed. Uranium had suddenly become war's most vital raw material. The miners hired to reopen Eldorado were screened by the RCMP and sworn to secrecy. The Western war chiefs feared an information leak that might prompt the Japanese to land a suicide battalion at Echo Bay. Later in the war, Tokyo Rose threatened just that in one of her jazz-and-insinuations broadcasts. Lord Haw-Haw also boasted that enemy agents would destroy "the secret Canadian war mine at Great Bear Lake".

What made the uranium suddenly so precious was that Allied scientists had discovered there was no need to spend a thousand years isolating an ounce of U_{235} with which to split the atom, as had been previously supposed. The large plutonium (U238) content of uranium was just as useful in releasing energy.

Uranium's importance was further underlined when on January 28, 1944, Howe, acting under wartime emergency powers, tabled an order-in-council in Ottawa, expropriating Eldorado's outstanding stock for $1.35 a share and transferring the company's assets to the Government. "I hope," he told the House of Commons, "that no questions will be asked until the necessity for withholding information no longer applies." The price paid for the stock was just a little higher than the closing market quote for the previous day's trading. The company's name was changed to Eldorado Mining & Refining (1944) Ltd.

LaBine remained president of the new government corporation, publicly undisturbed by the loss of the mine he had laboured so hard to bring into production. The Government spent millions enlarging the Echo Bay installations—money that could not have been raised from investors, who would have had to be kept in ignorance of the project's significance. But along Bay and St. James Streets shareholders groused about the injustice of the expropriation. U.S. stockholders petitioned for State Department intervention and threatened court action.

The denouement came with dramatic finality on August 6, 1945, when the atomic bomb burst over Hiroshima. The horror weapon's uranium, it was revealed, had come chiefly from Eldorado.

The news reactivated outraged protests from former Eldorado shareholders. A committee was set up in Chicago, headed by Anna Tamminga, a self-styled "eighty-four-year-old bedridden widow" who claimed that she had bought nine hundred Eldorado shares at $2.35 with her life savings. Howe called her "a non-existent fraud" and refused to answer her mail.

LaBine himself remains philosophical about the expropriation. "I haven't any regrets," he says. "Sure it was high-handed burglary. But it was war. After all, what you lose on oranges, you gain on bananas."

On November 1, 1945, John Diefenbaker, then a Conservative back-bencher, rose in the House of Commons to enquire sternly about the appointment of Grant Glassco, a Toronto chartered accountant, as investigator of Eldorado's radium and uranium transactions. Howe admitted that there was suspicion about the financial details of some Eldorado dealings both before and after expropriation. Glassco had been brought in to check sales and to ascertain the ultimate destination of all shipments.

Carl B. French, a former Eldorado secretary-treasurer, Dr. Marcel Pochon, the chemist in charge of the Port Hope refinery, and Boris Pregel, Eldorado's Russian-born sales agent in New York, were eventually charged with criminal conspiracy, involving unauthorized sales and the disappearance of some stocks of Eldorado ore, that had defrauded the company of $2.5 million since 1942. Civil action was substituted for the criminal charges in 1947, and the case was settled out of court, with a two-million-dollar payment by the accused.

LaBine was not named in connection with any of the charges. "Some people in our organization were disloyal and doing unethical things," he says. The full transcripts of Glassco's hearings have never been published.

The Government demonstrated its continuing faith in LaBine not only by keeping him in the Eldorado presidency, but by making him an Officer of the Order of the British Empire for his war work, and naming him a director of the Polymer Corporation, a Crown company making synthetic rubber at Sarnia, Ont.

Since Ottawa's expropriation, Eldorado under LaBine's guidance had been actively searching for other Canadian uranium deposits. LaBine sent twenty prospecting teams into the bush during the summer of 1944 with portable Geiger counters.

Within the next two years nearly two hundred radioactive sites were checked—many through extensive diamond drilling—but no new ore bodies were located until 1946. Einar Nelson and Phil St. Louis, two Eldorado prospectors, landed on Ace Lake near Lake Athabaska, in northern Saskatchewan, where a small pitchblende showing had been reported in 1932. When diamond drills confirmed the excited clicking of St. Louis' Geiger counter, a ridge between Ace Lake and Beaverlodge Lake was found to contain enough uranium to treble Canada's reserves. The government-owned company spent twenty million dollars establishing a second producer at Ace Lake in 1953. One of the Ace Mine drill holes intersected rock worth $417 a ton—the richest uranium ore ever discovered.

After Ottawa relaxed its monopoly on uranium prospecting, in 1947, LaBine resigned as the Eldorado president to continue the prospecting he had interrupted seventeen years before. "They never found anything after I left," he says with satisfaction.

He formed Nesbitt LaBine Uranium Mines in 1950, out of properties adjoining the Government's Beaverlodge workings. Two shafts were sunk and nearly a million dollars' worth of uranium was blasted out, but operations were suspended in 1956, because of insufficient mineralization at lower levels.

LaBine had meanwhile been dispatching prospecting parties all around the Nesbitt LaBine property—convinced, as he had been two decades earlier at Echo Bay, that he was in "elephant country". His hunch paid of spectacularly in August 1952, when Albert Zeemel, a prospector who had been on LaBine's payroll for twelve years, wired him: "Come quick. I've shot an elephant."

Zeemel had located outcrops near the St. Mary's Channel, twenty miles south-west of Beaverlodge, that made his Geiger counter chatter like a rural telephone line. By January of the next year, 173 diamond-drill holes had outlined a deposit fourteen hundred feet long and six hundred feet wide. Rich pay ore was distributed bacon-strip fashion, with fat and lean areas of occurrence. LaBine called his mine Gunnar, after a dormant gold mine he had floated in 1933.

The mine's uranium-concentrating mill went on tap at 11 A.M. on August 26, 1955, making Gunnar Canada's first private post-war uranium producer. The thirty-six months taken from staking to the first mill run stands as a speed record for a major Canadian mine. Gunnar shares, which could be bought for 23 cents in December 1952, hit $13.75 in the fall of 1953.

Only a dozen of Gunnar's 860 acres have so far been fully explored. But the value of the mine's established reserves is estimated at more than two hundred million dollars. The company's sales contracts guarantee a minimum net profit of eighteen million dollars by 1960. LaBine, as Gunnar's largest stockholder, is one of the Canadian mining industry's richest men. But he still insists on seeing every one of the many grubstake-hungry prospectors who shuffle into his office.

He talks to them for hours, reminiscing about the simpler, more exciting days in the bush. Those who tell a convincing story leave with money.

Joseph LaBine once tried to save his father's time by weeding out the obvious blue-sky dealers. But LaBine angrily stopped him. "You never can tell," he said. " My next visitor might be Saint Joseph."

chapter 8

THE STEINBERG BROTHERS

*"If a man goes without food for one day, he will lie.
If he goes without food for two days, he will steal.
If he goes without food for four days, he will riot and kill.
The food business
is the most essential in the world, and the largest."*

Economic change, like war, can be classed beyond that galaxy of human events whose course is determined by individual action. But the businessman who anticipates future trends and applies such theory to the daily evolution of his enterprise can become the pace-setter, not only in his trading area but for his industry.

The most spectacular example in Canada of uncommon economic clairvoyance of this kind is a family of five Montreal brothers, who have utilized their flashes of genius to parlay a coop-sized delicatessen into Canada's largest privately owned supermarket chain. Every thirty days during the past decade the Steinbergs have opened another monument to their prodigious merchandising artistry.

More than two million Canadians now wheel ten thousand shopping carts around the technicoloured shelves of the Steinberg supermarkets. At the end of World War II, the chain had twenty-four stores selling twelve million dollars' worth of goods. By 1963 the brothers expect to be operating two hundred units with turnover of nearly half a billion dollars. "We started with a philosophy, and we have carried it out," says Sam Steinberg, the second-eldest brother and company president. "The starting point was my mother's principle of keeping customers happy by giving them a little extra, and we haven't changed."

That sounds like an over-simplification, but Sam insists that his first reaction to tough problems is to ask himself: "What would mother have done?" then to act accordingly. A portrait of Ida Steinberg, a Jewish immigrant from Hungary, who started the business when she stocked a tiny Montreal shop with two hundred dollars' worth of groceries in 1917, hangs in the company board room where all important decisions are made.

The Steinbergs opened Quebec's first self-service store in 1934. They have since pioneered many of the selling methods now considered standard supermarket practice. Gerald Huxley, the retailing expert who heads the International Tea Bureau, calls them "The world's finest merchandisers". The company has won every retailing award available in North America.

The merchandising talent of the remarkable brothers has aroused such interest in the industry that three head-office employees spend most of their time acting as guides for visiting U.S. supermarket executives, who wish to examine more closely the ingredients of the Steinberg success.

One reason for the quintet's startling progress is that despite the number of brothers, cousins and other relatives in the business, promotion to greater responsibility depends much more on competence than on consanguinity. Ida Steinberg called Sam "the head" and Nathan "the heart" of the family. As vice-president of operations, Nathan is the company spokesman. Morris, the youngest brother, is in charge of promotion. Jack, the eldest, buys new equipment and bosses the maintenance department. Max, the least impulsive of the group, is vice-president and treasurer. Every share of the company's voting stock is owned by the family.

Sam is an unusual compromise of business acumen and social shyness. He can be the toughest of his tribe, but talks nearly always with apologetic politeness. His relaxations are bridge, pinochle and checkers, but these are only minor diversions in comparison to his fervently enjoyed family life. The brothers are all at work by 8 A.M. The business operates as a continual series of conferences.

The Steinbergs have from the beginning shown a compulsion for originality in a tradition-addicted industry. During the Depression they paid ten cents over the market price to farmers who delivered eggs the same day they were laid. Working with Gibson Craig of Canadian Industries Limited, they trebled sales of cheese and biscuits in 1937 by wrapping them in Cellophane. They were the first merchandisers in the world to use the transparent wrap for fruits and vegetables. They converted these departments to self-service as early as

1940. The year before they had set up parking lots for customers—then a rare convenience.

The vintage year for Steinberg-sponsored innovations was 1950, when conveyor-belt cashier stalls, magic-eye doors, and subsidized store-attached taxi services for customers were introduced. Three years later the unit at the Boulevard Shopping Centre near Montreal became the first supermarket in Canada with a "car order depot"—a hut on the parking lot, connected by underground conveyor belt to the check-out counters, where customers could have their groceries placed directly into car trunks.

Among the other conveniences for shoppers pioneered by the Steinbergs have been customer-operated coffee grinders, midget shopping carts for youngsters, vegetable scales that compensate for the weight of wrapping materials, customer lounges, merchandise bonuses for early-in-the-week shoppers, and one-way cart traffic to prevent nerve-jarring collisions among preoccupied housewives.

The brothers' insistence on buying the best produce at premium prices has had some peculiar results. At Montreal's Bonsecours market, farmers refuse to sell their vegetables and fruit until the Steinberg buyer has set the day's prices. To obtain field-fresh corn, Nathan Steinberg persuaded farmers near Montreal to pick the cobs at night. When they refused to work in the nocturnal dew among the high plants, the Steinbergs distributed truckloads of fishermen's rubber suits free to keep the vegetables flowing into their stores fresh at opening time.

To test their merchandise, the Steinbergs select goods from their own shelves for the head-office cafeteria. A panel of exacting housewives passes even stricter verdicts on every item before it's stocked regularly. Customer criticisms are scrupulously investigated, right down to the complaint of one fussy woman who threatened to boycott Steinberg's unless the Muzak played her favourite tunes.

A frisky advertising department headed by Ben Dobrinsky stimulates sales with many original gimmicks, including such useless but eye-catching bits of information as: "If all the tea chests received at Steinberg's in one year were placed one upon the other, they would reach a height approximately $5\frac{1}{2}$ times that of the Empire State Building." More earthy ads tout give-away contests, offer free grocery hampers for June brides, and push refresher courses in meal preparation.

Much of the sales promotion concentrates on creating a money-spending atmosphere on the sales floor. Each market has the gleaming appearance of a theatre foyer. The Steinbergs were the first to reject white as the traditional food-store color. They substituted a dynamic combination of tulip yellow, beige, green, burnt orange, and dark brown. Merchandise layout is planned to coincide with the typical housewife's shopping list.

The brothers breed their stores by mass production. At least half a dozen new units are constantly in the hatching process. Sites are picked by two probing Ph.D.'s—one a sociologist, the other an experimental physicist. Availability of land suggests many of the new locations, but more often a desirable trading area is spotted, then an appropriate plot sought. Opening of new units is an impressive exercise in hoopla, often lasting a week. The search for publicity gags at the cutting of the inaugural ribbon probably attained its climax in January, 1955, when Brother Sam smashed the ceremonial cord with high-energy gamma rays shot from a radioactive gun.

The rate of the chain's expansion is set by the training pace of the company's sales forces. Every new unit requires about seventy-five men and women, although increasing mechanization had raised the productivity of Steinberg labour so significantly that annual sales per man-hour increased 35 per cent between 1950 and 1955. Sydney Caplan, the company's director of personnel, has devised a scheme that allows department heads to nominate themselves for managership, whenever they feel qualified. When past performance bears out a self-recommendation, six months in a company management course precedes assignment to the first store. Nearly sixty of the company's store managers began as clerks. Their average age is 35; they earn $10,000 a year. Promotion is based on the ability to meet sales quotas.

The Steinbergs opened the first store outside Montreal in 1939, at Arvida, Quebec, following a request from housewives whose husbands were moved there by the Aluminum Company of Canada. In the summer of 1959, the Steinbergs purchased for a reported $50 million, the thirty-eight Ontario stores of Grand Union Limited. They have also established a few outlets in the Maritimes. "It is not impossible," says Nathan Steinberg, "that one day we will become national."

There is, in fact, only one location in Canada that will probably never have a Steinberg store. Remembering the friendly rivalry of the small shopkeepers in the upper section of Boulevard St. Laurent in Montreal, where Ida Steinberg opened her little delicatessen in 1917, the Steinbergs have vowed not to take away their business with a supermarket.

Ida Steinberg emigrated to Canada in 1911 from Debrecen in Hungary, where her husband had been a baker. Six years later she opened her store at 4419 boulevard St. Laurent in the district where most of the newcomers to the city had settled.

Sam's first after-school job was hawking papers at St. Catherine and Bleury. He set pins at bowling alleys in the evening, until he quit school at fourteen to help his mother. He won a delivery cart by sending in fifty Comfort Soap coupons, later he bought a chestnut pony called Nellie, and eventually he mechanized his rounds with a Model T truck. Sam and his brothers learned many of the selling tricks that have made them millionaires by watching their mother's early struggles.

The Steinberg grocery store was unique even in those humble days. Sam made his deliveries according to a posted schedule, instead of waiting for a full load to accumulate. Most of the stores in the neighbourhood had no attractive displays. Ida dressed up the narrow show-case and the interior with sales-influencing exhibits. Her apparent generosity in popping in a few extra apples or cookies into a customer's bag after she had weighed the paid-for amount was calculated to spread her reputation beyond the block's shoppers.

The size of the business was doubled in 1919, when Sam negotiated the rental of an adjoining store for sixty dollars a month. In order not to lose their customers who had moved to the more respectable Outremont district, in 1926 the family paid two thousand dollars for its first branch at 1271 Bernard Avenue. The business had expanded to four units when Steinberg Service Stores Limited was incorporated in 1930. Authorized capital was thirty-five thousand dollars, comprising 350 common shares, distributed among the family.

Financing of the growth that followed was entirely out of accumulated profits and bank overdrafts. Ida Steinberg managed the Monkland Avenue branch until 1939, when her only daughter married. She died at fifty-seven in 1942. Her husband, who had never taken an active part in the business, died five years later.

The decision that more than any other swung the Steinbergs toward business greatness was actually a desperate attempt to salvage the mistake made in 1933 of establishing a store at 2175 St. Catherine Street West. The location was so narrow that the conventional type of grocery counter would have projected into the fruit section, leaving almost no space for customers. Following several unsuccessful experiments, Sam closed the store on the last day of January 1934. Over the week-end he threw out all the sales counters except a small wrapping table near the exit. He changed the store's name to Steinberg's Wholesale Groceterias, slashed all his prices by 10 per cent and eliminated phone orders and credit.

On Monday morning, he opened Quebec's first self-service grocery store. Sales immediately shot up from four thousand to ten thousand dollars a month. The customers tried to lug away so much merchandise that the Steinbergs recruited a gang of neighbourhood children with wagons to deliver for a nickel any purchase of three dollars or more. The new selling method caught on so well that all the units were converted to self-service. By 1937, the family was operating twenty-two stores with a turnover of $3,365,491.

Not everyone was happy about the shopping revolution. With the art of salesmanship largely eliminated, most of the clerks who had built up large personal followings left to join more conservative employers. One muscular customer became so enraged when he was asked to serve himself that he grabbed Sam by the collar and shook him almost into insensibility. Many others cussed the Steinberg store managers, and vowed they would never return. Sam helped them to come back without losing face, by switching all his unit managers to new locations.

During the three years before the outbreak of World War II, the Steinbergs built nine small supermarkets—the first was at 5820 Monkland Avenue in Montreal. Canadian banks then considered them such poor risks that they would lend money for the ventures only if Sam agreed to build apartments above the stores. That way every mortgage could be at least partly protected in case the market failed.

Sam was by this time almost completely absorbed with policy matters, but he set aside his mornings to tour the chain and chat with customers. He would deliver their orders on his way to inspect the next outlet. His managers were instructed to prod sales by telephoning housewives with news of special bargains. Sam made price deals with wholesalers by having trucks call each morning at their warehouses, saving them transport costs and getting job-lot prices. Staple goods were arranged at the back of each store, so that to reach them customers had to pass the commodities usually bought on impulse

The proportion of non-food merchandise increased so rapidly that by 1953 the company was selling six thousand items, compared with two thousand in 1937. The trend is continuing. "Eventually," says Nathan Steinberg, "our supermarkets will become department stores."

The Steinbergs plan to introduce, among other things, banks of vending machines to line store fronts at night for selling basic foods, and an automatic check-out system that calculates a customer's bill by electronically scanning the prices marked on goods in slightly radioactive ink. (A possibility of the future is that the remarkable gadgets of science may be enlisted to trap shoplifters. Concealed devices at store exits will set off jangling alarms when they spot the extra bulge under the shopper's coat as a can of beans she is trying to sneak out.)

Moving aisles, television ordering stations on parking lots and the irradiation of steaks for permanent freshness are among future possibilities. Long display cases may be re-grouped so that customers will unavoidably encounter self-moving displays demonstrating the application of new products.

The Steinbergs, however, will remain primarily merchants of food. "If a man goes without food for one day, he will lie," says Brother Nathan. "If he goes without food for two days, he will steal. If he goes without food for four days, he will riot and kill. The food business is the most essential in the world, and the largest."

Such is the commodious philosophy of the Steinberg brothers in their high-powered quest to lure more and more Canadians into spending their food dollars in the flossy palaces they have erected for that very purpose.

chapter 9

DR. HANS LUNDBERG

*A plump and witty Norseman,
he stomps through each day with the courtly manners
of a politician continually announcing
popular legislation. His bald head,
packed with talent equally recognized in the worlds of
business and of science,
ends in a luxuriant eyebrow thatch that shields the
stubbornness of his blue eyes.*

WHENEVER Dr. Hans Torkel Frederik Lundberg finds the
time to plop himself down behind the massive green leather
desk in his Toronto office, he surreptitiously winks up at a
plaster guardian angel suspended from the ceiling. The
figurine is conventional enough from the visitor's end of the
desk. But the side of the angel facing Lundberg has its

cherubic countenance permanently twisted into an open-mouthed expression of admiration for its keeper.

The angel's attitude of heavenly awe is eminently justified.

In his obsessive rummaging through the crust of four continents, Lundberg has discovered minerals worth at least six billion dollars—more than any other prospector in Canadian history. Easily the world's most successful treasure hunter, Lundberg has also traced the gold sources of King Solomon, the Roman Empire, and the Incas. He is the discoverer of the ice-age skeleton that provided proof of man's existence in the western hemisphere fifteen thousand years ago. While he has not quite realized the ancient dreams of the alchemists, he has scientifically established his ability to grow gold, and operates the world's first gold farm.

A plump and witty Norseman, Lundberg stomps through each day with the courtly manners of a politician continually announcing popular legislation. His bald head, packed with talent equally recognized in the worlds of business and of science, ends in a luxuriant eyebrow thatch that shields the stubbornness of his blue eyes. The fair Nordic skin of his face glows with the unyielding intensity of the man, producing the pink complexion of a champion skier.

In the thirty-six years since he came to Canada from Sweden, Lundberg has become recognized as the free world's most experienced practitioner of airborne geophysics. This is the inexact science of using instruments mounted in aircraft to feel out new mines by gauging the magnetism, gravitational pull, radioactivity, and other physical properties of rock formations as much as two thousand feet underground. His gadget-studded aircraft troll for minerals, much as an angler catches trout.

Although he holds many off-beat views, Lundberg is so highly regarded by fellow scientists that he has read seventy-five papers before learned societies all over the world, and was chosen to deliver a major address to the 1949 United Nations Scientific Conference on the conservation and utilization of resources. "Lundberg is a real genius," says John W. Carrington, editor of *The Northern Miner*. "He is the father of geophysical prospecting."

To direct the world-wide field operations of his company, Lundberg Explorations Limited, he travels more than sixty thousand miles a year—most of it by air. Lundberg's mineral surveys are carried out under contract for mining companies. "I usually lose interest when shaft-sinking starts," he says.

His aerial gadgets have found new mines in twenty-eight countries, as well as every geologically favourable region of Canada. He has been associated with the discovery or extension of such well-known Canadian mines as Buchans, Amulet, McIntyre Porcupine, Siscoe, Granby Consolidated, Toburn, Falconbridge, Stadacona, Rouyn, Bevcourt, Opemiska, Rainville, Copper Mountain, Donalda, D'Eldona, and several Noranda, International Nickel, and Ventures subsidiaries. In 1942 he outlined deposits of cryolite, essential for the manufacture of aluminum, in a secret war mission to Greenland. In 1949 his air crews skimmed over the Cariboo district of British Columbia, locating hidden channels in placer-gold streams. In 1952 he helped the U.S. Atomic Energy Commission find uranium deposits in Colorado.

One recent discovery of a Lundberg airborne magnetometer crew was the billion-ton iron-ore body on the Belcher Islands, in Hudson Bay. "Anyone can run a magnetometer," says Douglas Banks, president of the Belcher Mining Corporation, which developed the find, "but damn few can interpret its findings like Lundberg." Bob Jowsey, one of Canada's most successful mining men, who often hires Lundberg, says: "As an explorer, he has been ahead of anybody I know. He's a great pioneer."

Lundberg's pioneering instincts are never more apparent than when he's telling a doubting audience about his unique gold-growing experiments. His technique consists simply of harvesting plants that extract the gold from the earth through their roots and concentrate it in their leaves. "Underground waters in millions of years carry upward slight, dissolved traces of the minerals they touch," he explains. "The plants soak up this moisture, but the minerals are poison to their system. To protect themselves, they capsule the metal at the ends of their leaves." Lundberg has refined gold out of the ashes of the leaves, most successfully from the tufts of the common horsetail—a pale brown weed, about ten inches high, that grows in sandy or gravelly soil in many parts of Canada. Near Timmins he has burned as much as four ounces of gold (worth $140) out of a ton of horsetails. Lundberg now grows the weeds over low-grade gold deposits in northern Indiana and Illinois, strengthening his claim to the title of history's first gold farmer.

One of his greatest prospecting contributions has been Lundberg's introduction to Canada of vegetation sampling as a guide to underground minerals. "It is definitely possible," he says, "to go out into an unknown area and, from a study of certain plants or trees, determine not only approximately where ore is to be found, but also what metals there may be in it." He has analyzed plants to track down lead, manganese, vanadium, molybdenum, tungsten, tin, silver, and copper mineralization as much as fifty feet underground, and once helped an associate find a chromium mine in Greece by the long-distance study of leaves from the area's scrubby oaks.

When he's plant-prospecting, Lundberg picks about six hundred vegetation samples per square mile, at fifty-foot intervals in straight lines across the property. He looks for needles, leaves or branches at similar heights from the same plant family. Lab technicians analyze the specimen by burning them before a spectroscope, the astronomer's instrument for unravelling the elements of starlight.

Once he visited a farmer north of Kingston, Ont., whose maple syrup was being rejected by U.S. border officials because of its high lead content. He toured the farm, sampling tree branches. Through a leaf analysis he eventually located a small deposit of lead. It wasn't enough for commercial mining, but he was able to mark the trees directly above the ore body. By not tapping them, the farmer has since got his maple syrup past Customs.

While he enjoys forays of this kind, Lundberg now spends most of his time at his Toronto headquarters scribbling interpretations on the geophysical charts brought in by his field teams. His thirty-odd head-office employees address their boss as "Dr. Lundberg", but in the coffee room he's affectionately known as "Father". This paternal instinct reflects more than friendly esteem. For thanks to Lundberg's instruments, the office staff consists of the richest clerks and stenographers in the country.

During a geophysical survey flight into claims near James Bay in 1953, Lloyd Leach, Lundberg's director of field operations, noticed a parallel bend in two rivers north of

Kapuskasing, Ontario, which to him indicated that a solid rock mass—possibly with ore in it—lay between them. The aircraft's geophysical detection gear registered such a kick that he turned it on during ensuing flights and eventually blocked out a strong iron-ore indication.

Leach collected twenty thousand dollars from the office staff to have the claims staked. Another office collection was taken up to finance diamond drilling, which outlined a hundred million tons of iron ore. The Steel Company of Canada bought the claims in April 1956 for a million dollars, giving the staff syndicate a better than forty-to-one pay-off. To Lundberg, the most satisfying outcome of the office bonanza was that none of his "millionaires" resigned.

Lundberg usually leaves the office early, but he always packs a briefcase home. He travels in a rented, chauffeur-driven limousine. He hates driving; his own 1952 Chrysler sits inactive on blocks in his garage.

The geophysicist spends most of his leisure time enlarging his stamp collection. "Stamps," he says, "are a study in history, printing and geography. To me, they're something alive." His two hundred albums, stored inside a walk-in safe tucked behind a false living-room panel, include stamps from letters carried on many of the sixty balloon ascents out of Paris during the 1870 German siege. "Lundberg," according to Douglas Patrick, a leading Canadian stamp authority, "is Canada's only consistent gold-medal-winner in international philatelic competitions."

As well as four medals for stamps, Lundberg has two Swedish scientific gold medals. Gustav VI, King of Sweden, personally created him a Doctor of Technology, one of the country's highest scientific distinctions. Although he has several times been offered a Swedish title, it is an honour he can't accept, because he has been a Canadian citizen since 1937.

His home is a luxurious eight-room bungalow on a fashionable dead-end street in north Toronto. The elevated lot and flat-roof design were originally meant to adapt the house for helicopter landings, but the idea was never implemented. The basement is split into three large weaving rooms where Lundberg's wife—the former Signe Sjoberg, a high-school sweetheart—works at her five looms spinning rugs and draperies. She bases some of her patterns on her husband's geophysical maps, giving her products surrealistic originality.

The home's main hall is lined with Lundberg's library, containing mostly technical books in eight languages. He speaks and reads Russian, French, German, Spanish, Danish and Norwegian, as well as Swedish and English. Off his bedroom is one of Lundberg's secret indulgences—a yellow-and-blue-tiled bathroom with a closed-in glass shower-bath compartment. It has indirect fluorescent lights that switch on automatically when he steps in for a dip.

In his living-room there is a shelf of petrified tree chips and fossils. They are the souvenirs of Lundberg's archaeological man-hunt on the clay bottom of dried-up Lake Texcoco, near Mexico City. Previous searches had turned up elephant bones in the region and bits of worked stone that indicated that man had hunted there during the late ice age. Human remains were needed to prove the archaeologists' argument that man inhabited this continent long before the predecessors of the American Indians crossed over from Asia.

Lundberg flew to Mexico in February 1947, with the theory that there had been time for the skeletons to mineralize, making them detectable by his instruments. The first two of the three spots he marked for digging contained nothing but pools of water. In the third—three and a half feet down—lay the oldest human skeleton unearthed in the western hemisphere. The fifteen-thousand-year-old cranium had pronounced eyebrow ridges set in a low, vaulted forehead. Ninety pits were dug after Lundberg left but no other bone remains were found.

The discovery of the Tepexpan Man, as the find is known, was not Lundberg's first venture into prospecting for the unusual. In 1937 he took his instruments to a mile-wide crater near Canyon Diablo in northern Arizona, to seek a missing meteorite. From the size of its crater, it was thought to have weighed more than a million tons, and from the odd fragments found, it was known to have consisted of ninety-two per cent iron, making it worth roughly twenty million dollars. Shafts sunk 650 feet below the crater had found no trace of the heavenly rock.

Lundberg dismissed the traditional approach of looking for the meteorite beneath its crater. He believed that it had hit an underground lake, boiling it into steam, and that the ensuing explosion had scattered the meteoritic material horizontally around the crater. Some three thousand feet from the crater's centre, his gear picked up a strong indication of iron ore.

When he revealed his find in New York, an elderly heiress offered him eight hundred thousand dollars for a few tons of the meteorite. "I want to build a church," she explained. "I want to build the only church in the world that will be made of material direct from heaven." Lundberg was tempted, but

Arizona turned the crater region into a state park before a shaft could confirm his discovery.

His reputation for unconventional prospecting has prompted many treasure hunters to seek his services. Just before World War II he directed a search for a sunken ship off the Bahamas that was supposed to have a hold full of silver bullion. Lundberg located the wreck, but its cargo turned out to be bars of lead.

In 1940 he organized an expedition into the Peruvian Andes to look for Inca gold. It was financed by his friend Dr. Axel Wenner-Gren, the controversial Swedish financier who was later granted a prospecting concession over one-tenth of British Columbia.

Instead of looking for hidden Inca treasures as previous explorers had done, Lundberg searched for the source of the ancient race's gold. The sixty-seven-member party found two lost Inca cities—Sayaq Marka and Phoyu Pata Marka— and at the foot of a great cliff abandoned gold pits were discovered. But the terrain was too dangerous and the natives too unfriendly for more detailed investigation.

At the head of the Manu River the expedition stumbled on a bizarre white colony, which had been founded by a prospector sent into Peru by Henry Ford in 1907 to plant rubber trees. The eighty-year-old patriarch, who had thirty-three years earlier chosen jungle life instead of attempting a return to civilization, had only three requests. He wanted a bag of salt to season his diet, a meat grinder to help overcome the loss of his teeth, and the services of the expedition's Peruvian priest to baptize his children. He balked at the priest's entreaties to let himself be married, but the baptizing took ten hours. The old man had ninety descendants.

Lundberg's company was also involved in a search for the fabled gold mines of King Solomon. On the basis of aerial photographs and surveys taken by one of Lundberg's associates, a British mining syndicate in 1935 found some ancient gold workings two hundred and fifty miles north-east of Jidda, in Saudi Arabia, thought to have been the source of the Biblical king's treasures. No further mining was carried out, but piles of waste surrounding the pits had been so primitively processed that a mill set up by the company extracted seventeen dollars' worth of gold from every ton of tailings.

Lundberg's strangest quest was not for gold, but for champagne. At the end of prohibition he located forty cases of champagne that had been buried in the garden of a Long Island estate. The wine had arrived just as the owner was called away on a sudden trip to Paris. A gardener, who had buried the shipment for safekeeping, died of pneumonia during the owner's absence and left no map. Lundberg tuned his geophysical gear to the "ting" of champagne bottles by having friends hide empties.

He now has little time for treasure hunting, but admits he'd like to explore Oak Island, in Mahone Bay south of Halifax, the rumoured site of Captain Kidd's gold cache. He has also studied Canada's two major diamond rushes—to Val d'Or, Quebec, in 1950 and to the Eastmain River near James Bay in 1909—and has worked out his own theory. He believes there may be diamonds in the throats of such extinct volcanoes as Mount Royal in the centre of Montreal, and nearby Mount Oka. He once started poking around Mount Oka, but the Trappist monks who own the land chased him away.

Stalking diamonds and pirate gold help nourish the mad-cap side of Lundberg's make-up, which he first demonstrated, with almost fatal results, as a teen-ager in his native Malmo, a southern Swedish port community. He built a set of wings out of bamboo spars joined by wrapping paper, and headed for a cliff from which he intended to glide into the sea. Some trees entangled the contraption, halting his plunge but cracking his collarbone.

Cured of his aerial ambitions, Lundberg enrolled in the mining-engineering course at the Royal Institute of Technology at Stockholm. His studies were interrupted by a short stint in the ski regiment that guarded the Swedish–Finnish border during World War I. In 1915 he was stranded for six months while exploring coal deposits in the Arctic Spitsbergen Islands.

He became an assistant mining professor at the Royal Institute in 1917, but spent his summers in the field. In an isolated northern Swedish village he once interviewed a Lapp witch doctor, awaiting trial for killing patients by having them sniff the fumes from his secret potion. Lundberg's tests showed that the brew was arseno-pyrite—the source of fatal arsenic, but also of copper. At the spot where the witch doctor had been mixing his deadly tonic, Lundberg used his first invention—a crude electric magnetometer—to discover the main ore body of what later became the huge Kristineberg mine. It made Sweden independent of copper imports during World War II and is still a major producer.

During the next five years Lundberg pioneered many geophysical techniques in successful mineral hunts throughout western Europe and northern Africa. In 1920, while trying to probe an impassable bog in northern Sweden, he suspended his instruments from a kite and took the first air-borne geophysical readings in history. In northern Spain, a year later, he discovered the long-sought—though largely worked out—mines that provided the ancient Roman Empire with most of its gold.

By 1923 the reputation of the young Swedish geophysicist and his omniscient instruments had crossed the Atlantic. August Hecksher, a New York financier, offered Lundberg $125 a day for six months to find him new mines. His first recollection of North America is having a Thanksgiving Day dinner in New York's Pennsylvania Hotel. He had been taught not to leave anything on his plate, but the steaks were far too big.

Lundberg worked out the agreement without spectacular success, then formed his own exploration company. He located a small base-metal ore body in Cobalt in 1924 and was so impressed with the country's mineral potential that he decided to settle in Canada permanently.

One of his first major strikes was at the Buchans River Mine, a small and gradually petering out lead-zinc property near Red Indian Lake in central Newfoundland. The company didn't want to gamble too much money on Lundberg's still unproven gadgets, so it limited his prospecting contract to one square mile. After briefly walking around the property, he decided to lug his instruments into a patch of swamp, west of the little shaft. The bog swarmed with blackflies, and the humming induction coils of his electrical gear attracted wild bears out of the surrounding bush. They paced hungrily around the machines, convinced they were camouflaged beehives.

Lundberg ordered a trench dug four thousand feet west of

the shaft, where his earphones had registered their strongest kick. The miners cursed Lundberg for the apparently senseless burrowing through the syrupy muck. Fifty feet down they exposed outcroppings of the then richest lead-zinc deposit in the world. Buchans is still mining Lundberg's discovery; more than a billion dollars' worth of ore has been taken from under the swamp.

Even after this spectacular affirmation of his powers Lundberg had to fight for the recognition of geophysics among Canadian mining men. The science was too new, not always effective, and there were many charlatans. Although he continued to find ore bodies more regularly than any pick-and-shovel prospector in the country, many of his early clients thought of Lundberg as just a lucky Swede with a hopped-up divining rod. In 1928 the Canadian Institute of Mining and Metallurgy asked the government to investigate the value of geophysics by tests over a known mineral site. Of the two dozen "geophysicists" who accepted the challenge, only Lundberg and one other candidate were able to outline the ore body.

Finally in 1929, the American Institute of Mining & Metallurgical Engineers allowed him ten minutes to address its New York meeting. "And with no discussion period," Lundberg ruefully recalls. His early professional relations were stormy because he was so often proved right after contradicting the advice of geologists and mining engineers. At a base-metal mine near Bourlamaque, Quebec, now known as Golden Manitou, geologists forecast ore extensions east of the shaft. Lundberg advised a drive westward. The richest ore was found in the western zone, after an eastward exploration found only scattered values.

At the Windpass Gold Mine, fifty miles north of Kamloops, B.C., underground exploration had not lived up to encouraging surface showings. Lundberg outlined a new exploration pattern. After boring through a hundred feet of barren rock, drills bit into a million-dollar gold vein.

At the great Falconbridge nickel mine near Sudbury, engineers had been unable to sink a new shaft without having it swamped by quicksand. Lundberg picked a knoll of solid crust and predicted bedrock a hundred feet down. Drilling confirmed his depth estimate to within six inches.

Some of Lundberg's early searches into regions of Canada once considered bare of minerals have taken more than twenty years to be confirmed. He was the first geophysicist into the Chibougamau area of northern Quebec, where in 1936 he outlined the copper deposits mined twenty years later by Copper Rand Chibougamau.

In 1938 he found a boulder with rich zinc-lead-copper values at Armstrong Brook, west of Bathurst, New Brunswick, near the site of the spectacular 1953 base-metals strike. Convinced that the rock had been separated from its mother lode by glacier movements, he traced the boulder for nineteen miles back to the Tetagouche River, where he outlined an impressive ore body. The property was developed in 1954 by New Calumet, a Ventures Limited subsidiary.

Lundberg remains a scientific rebel. He loves to ridicule the *scientissimo* geophysicists—his label for colleagues who try to present the profession as a mysterious super-science. He constantly urges the wider adoption of geophysics by practical prospectors, and once compared the science to cooking.

"Ninety per cent of our best cooks," he told the 1942 meeting of the American Institute of Mining Engineers, "use baking powder without the slightest concern over the molecular changes that may result in the cake . . . the mistakes of practical people using geophysical methods are not more frequent than those of the theoretically skilled scientists." The Institute was so shocked that his paper was "misplaced" and not published with the session's regular transcripts.

Lundberg regards geophysics as more of an art than a science. "Dame Nature," he says, "is a creature of such infinite variety that attempts to reproduce her moods artificially can never be wholly successful."

Lundberg's main contributions to his science have been his adaptations of geophysical instruments for use from the air. He has redesigned the supersensitive gadgets to operate from the shaky dashboards of small aircraft, and has completely restudied the techniques of interpreting results. Twenty of his inventions have been patented.

He caused a sensation among petroleum men when he introduced his scintillation aerial prospecting method to Texas oil fields in 1950. He found one well in Dawson County that still brings him royalties of $25,000 a year. Venezuela now fixes its oil-bearing-land auction prices according to his surveys. His instruments helped discover the Coleville oil and gas field in western Saskatchewan, as well as parts of the Redwater field in Alberta.

The next phase in Lundberg's assault on the earth's minerals may involve the ocean. He is particularly interested in seaweed beds off Ireland which he believes may be capturing uranium out of seawater in recoverable quantities.

Whichever direction Lundberg's future probing takes, his activities are bound to involve him in more controversy. When he announced his plant-sampling method, for instance, one crusty prospector objected in a letter to *The Northern Miner*: "I wonder what the Ontario Securities Commission would say, if I put out a prospectus stating that the Balm of Gilead on my claims has a high copper content. Some of those scientists should work out a method employing the beaver to go prospecting. Chewing leaves and bark is his business. Then we could sample the beaver and other animals for values. Skunks should run high."

"Yes," says Lundberg. "That's not impossible." With a dreamy smile of scientific delectation, he tells the story of a mine in Rhodesia, discovered by tracing the copper flecks in a parrot's tail feathers.

chapter 10

DONALD GORDON

"Nobody ever did anything by pussy-footing."

THE first thing you notice about Donald Gordon is his hands. Their movements are never aimless. In their welcoming grip you feel the granite determination that hoisted him from a dollar-a-day factory flunkey to the presidency of the world's greatest railway empire.

The Canadian National Railways, guided by these hands, is Canada's largest corporation. Nearly 35,000 miles of track make it the world's longest railroad. With 113,000 on its payroll, the C.N.R. is easily Canada's biggest employer. In fact, only thirteen Canadian cities have a larger population.

To operate the government-owned C.N.R., Donald Gordon is paid $5,800 a month—roughly twice as much as the Prime Minister of Canada.

Gordon, an unlovely owl-eyed giant of a Scot, had no educational or family advantage. At twenty-three he was the youngest bank inspector in the country, and by thirty-seven the Deputy Governor of the Bank of Canada. Then, as chairman of the Wartime Prices & Trade Board, he was the economic dictator of this nation at war.

He has advanced by not dealing with business problems in the approved manner of meeting them half-way. He collides with them. "I treat each new situation with spontaneous ingenuity," he explains.

He is no fonder of money than any other Scotchman. But he does love power. "Nobody," he says, "ever did anything by pussy-footing."

His definition of the ideal executive is one who decides to do the impossible, then hires assistants to carry out his orders. Recognized by the world's railroading fraternity as one of its shrewdest members, Gordon in his daily routine touches almost every human occupation. He must make decisions as a real-estate broker, engineer, caterer, economist, architect, lawyer, mechanic, publicist, hotel manager, and too often as a lay father confessor. He holds the most difficult and frustrating presidency in Canadian business.

Instead of having a finite number of shareholders to satisfy, he must report annually through Parliament to all Canadians, who as taxpayers have for nearly forty years been paying his road's massive deficits. He can't get rough with the airlines—his main competition—because Trans-Canada, the largest of them, is one of his own subsidiaries. He must battle the Canadian Pacific for every passenger and pound of freight, but at the same time remind himself that his own rates are set by the Board of Transport Commissioners, which uses C.P.R. profits as its yardstick.

Gordon's office, on the fifth floor of the C.N.R.'s Montreal headquarters, is the size of a small railway station. He strides in past his various executive assistants, private secretaries and associate private secretaries precisely at nine; he rarely leaves before seven.

His day is partitioned into exact time intervals for each visitor, set in advance by his senior staff. At the end of each allotted period, an assistant soundlessly appears with the next caller. Casual well-wishers who want to chat are relentlessly ushered along within five minutes. Gordon is obsessed with punctuality. During his wartime stint in Ottawa he complained that he wasted more time by being on time than any man in the country.

"Gordon is a tireless worker," said James Ilsley, who was then Finance Minister. "But he is totally devoid of that stolidity which enables some men to work all the time, because they work like horses. Calmness is not one of his outstanding characteristics."

To help him picture the problems of his railroad, Gordon has invented an electrically operated six-foot-square map on which any part of the system may be made to light up by pressing the appropriate button. He travels twenty thousand miles a year in the *Bonaventure*, the private car converted for him at a cost of $127,000. His field visits are spaced so that he covers the entire rail network every thirty-six months.

For relaxation, he leafs through the occasional whodunit or historical novel; putters uncomfortably in the basement of his house as a not-too-handy amateur carpenter; and plays bridge, according to one frequent partner, "more argumentatively than brilliantly."

Gordon is happiest when drinking Scotch and reminiscing with half a dozen confrères from the Wartime Prices & Trade Board. By midnight he is usually bellowing almost proper Scottish folk songs in a lusty baritone, joyously accompanying himself on an undersized concertina.

He often retreats to his 150 acres of virgin bush at Lustre Lake, twenty miles north of Ottawa. There he has a comfortable main cottage, plus a bizarre guarantee of privacy. It's a floating hut shaped like a Dutch windmill, anchored to a rocky outcrop on his lake. The mill's interior is just large enough for Gordon's six-foot-six cot. He has often dozed here, a fishing line tied to his big toe, and caught pike through the wooden island's trap-door.

In town, Gordon dresses conservatively in dark blue or grey suits, but he cheats in his evening wear by using a shop shirt with formal-collar attachment. His clothes are constantly being dislocated by the size of the man—he's 6′ 4½″ tall, and his weight shuttles between 240 and 270 pounds. His chest measurement is forty-eight inches on the exhale. He doesn't get up from a seat, rather he unfolds himself. His walk is the shamble of a bear on the way from hibernation.

Gordon has discovered that on the speaker's platform he can combine relaxation with work. He enjoys giving up to sixteen speeches a year, poised as rigid as a drillmaster behind the lectern, both hands in the side pockets of his coat and only glancing at his text.

His humour is sharp and natural. "We have had reports from some animal lovers," he once told a Canadian Club luncheon, "that during mating season the bull moose has mistaken the sound of our diesel klaxon for the vocal response of an amorous cow moose—with results that have been disastrous to the male animal." Referring to the many lawsuits filed against his railway, he remarked that nothing improves the value of a cow so much as to cross it with a C.N.R. locomotive.

To a Toronto audience of travelling salesmen he once apologized for not starting with a joke about farmers' daughters. "Unfortunately," he said, "I find that my stock of these is rather low. For this I can suggest only two explanations : either there are fewer commercial travellers on the road these days, or there aren't as many farmers' daughters as there used to be. No one in this audience can possibly accept the first suggestion, so I leave you to ponder upon the second and to mourn its implications."

His favourite story concerns the president of a well-known U.S. railroad whom he calls Mr. Black. There walked into his office one day an Irishman, hat on, pipe in mouth, who said : "I want a pass to St. Louis."

"Who are you?" demanded the startled president.

"I'm Pat Casey, one of your switchmen," was the reply.

Black, thinking this was a good time to teach proper company etiquette, said: "Now, Pat, I'm not going to say that I will refuse your request, but there are certain forms a man should observe. You should knock at the door, and when I say 'Come in' you should enter, take your hat off, and removing your pipe, ask: 'Are you President Black?' I would say, 'I am, who are you?' Then you would tell me your name and I would ask 'What can I do for you?' Then you would make your request and the matter would be settled. Now you go out and come in again and see if you can't do it better."

Two hours later in came Casey, with his hat off and the pipe out of his mouth. "Good morning," he said, "are you President Black?"

"I am. Who are you?"

"I'm Pat Casey, one of your switchmen."

"Well Mr. Casey, and what can I do for you?"

"You can go to hell. I got a job and a pass on the Wabash."

Gordon once startled a group of Montreal railroaders by addressing them as "fellow ferro-equinologists"—a term he concocted for "those interested in the lore of the iron horse." His own passion for railroading was sudden and involuntary.

The federal government, late in 1949, decided to assign to Gordon, its ace wartime trouble-shooter, the tough job of cutting the railway's deficit and raising the morale of its employees. He had no qualifications beyond the mulish organizational skill with which he had run Canada's wartime economy, and an established zest for new challenges.

At his press conferences as a neophyte railway chief,

Gordon admitted to only one firm opinion about railroading: men of his dimensions couldn't fit into sleeping-car berths. On the first day of his new job in Montreal he spoke over a national radio hookup, presented his respects to Roman Catholic Archbishop Joseph Charbonneau, sipped tea with Anglican Bishop John Dixon, then addressed Montreal's leading businessmen at the Saint James's Club. "I want all you gentlemen to call me up for free transportation, free telegraph facilities and free hotel rooms," he said. "I can assure you that no request will be declined more promptly, nor with more regret."

Gordon learned to use his ignorance as an efficiency weapon while probing the anatomy of his railway. His persistent "Why do you do it that way?" often helped expose obsolete methods. "Studying a railway problem," he discovered, 'is like looking into a microscope to watch the development of a single-celled creature which multiplies by dividing itself in two, then both halves divide in turn, and so on." His biggest shock was a travel survey he ordered to determine public attitude toward the C.N.R. It showed that out of a hundred, eight Canadian adults had never ridden on a train.

The inaugural year at C.N.R. was the most difficult in Gordon's life. His wife died alone in their Windsor Hotel room, three months after he became president. One of his best vice-presidents died; another retired. Floods and landslides destroyed sections of track in the West and the Maritimes. A strike-inspired coal shortage forced him to cut passenger services. The dispute with the non-operating railway unions culminated in the country's first rail strike. This succession of crises permanently blunted Gordon's temperament.

In the age of the automobile and the airplane, most railroad presidents regard their passengers as secondary cargo, but few say so as bluntly as Gordon. He defines passengers as the most articulate and the least remunerative commodity carried on his trains. "I am continually amazed," he says, "to see how communities which consistently fail to patronize our services can marshal such eloquent arguments about our indispensability the moment abandonment is contemplated." *The Wiarton Echo* once editorialized: "The C.N.R. has proposed that the passenger trains from Palmerston to Kincardine be suspended, as they are not paying their way. Since when has the C.N.R. started worrying about a few more bucks in the red? Must be Donald Gordon, the tightwad."

Original Gordon directives to reduce dining-car losses have included smaller plates to make steaks look bigger and cutting worn tablecloths into napkins. He ordered that the used soap bars be collected out of emptied sleeping cars, for use in washing down passenger equipment.

To take what he calls "the chief clerkism" out of the company, Gordon set up a staff college for the grooming of future executives and revamped promotion procedures. During the decade after World War II, the C.N.R. spent $86 million building six hundred miles of rail to reach mineral discoveries. This represented more new trackage than has been added by any railway in the Western Hemisphere during the post-war period.

No Canadian railway president before Donald Gordon has been threatened with lynching and petitioned against to the

Queen of England. Such fierce resentment climaxed the C.N.R.'s 1954 decision to use the name Queen Elizabeth for its new $24 million hotel in Montreal.

Mayor Jean Drapeau labelled the choice as inexcusable effrontery to French Canadians. "How would Toronto people like it," he fumed, "if the C.N.R. built a hotel there and called it Le Louis-Joseph Papineau?" Fifteen volumes of protest petitions with a quarter of a million signatures were sent to federal cabinet ministers. Seventy-nine Quebec municipal councils passed resolutions demanding that the hotel be named Le Château Maisonneuve, after the founder and first governor of Montreal.

When the Queen visited Ottawa in the fall of 1957, a petition was hurled into the royal limousine as she was leaving Christ Church Cathedral, begging consent to the withdrawal of her name. "This problem," the document reads, "threatens to lower your prestige among us." A few months earlier, it had taken seventy-five Montreal policemen to disperse four hundred students rioting under Gordon's office windows. They had threatened to hang him, and tore to shreds his straw-stuffed effigy.

It's not generally known that Gordon wasn't responsible for picking the controversial name. Several names had been discussed in his office. The Queen Elizabeth and Le Château Maisonneuve were among them. It was decided to enquire informally about the legal procedure necessary in each case.

As part of this correspondence, Governor-General Vincent Massey was asked about the formalities required for use of the Queen's name. The Governor-General was in

England at the time. He was so delighted with the idea that he promptly asked the Queen. She was equally delighted and gave her permission. Suddenly it had become too late to make a change without insulting the monarchy. Gordon loyally swallowed all the blame and whooped like an Indian brave at the hotel's official opening, as he placed a redskin feather headdress on Hollywood columnist Hedda Hopper.

Gordon's moustache bristles an anger warning when visitors joke about the Queen Elizabeth episode. He's equally furious if they refer to his railway as a socialist enterprise. "That's unadorned nonsense," he insists. He maintains that the C.N.R. is operated with the same profit motives as a private corporation. "Exhortations from an executive are a poor substitute for the discipline of a profit-and-loss account, without which administrative problems are robbed of both urgency and clarity," he says.

Legally a civil servant, Gordon treats his job with the free-wheeling independence of a colonial governor who gives a stewardship of his actions once a year to distant and uninformed officials. His annual collisions with parliamentary committees make spicy reading. He once bet Chester McLure, a Prince Edward Island Conservative, a dinner at the parliamentary restaurant that the C.N.R. *did* have enough refrigerator cars on the Island, and lost.

During one clash in 1953, he banged his desk and spluttered at Opposition members of the railway committee : "Do you think that Jack Pickersgill (then secretary to the Cabinet) can scare *me*?" Davie Fulton, the brilliant Conservative who later became Minister of Justice, shot back : "And do *you* think you can scare ME?" Another time when senators complained that they could not sleep on the Toronto–Ottawa run, Gordon sarcastically suggested they fortify themselves with Scotch first.

Despite his dependence on Government policy, Gordon often attacks the Railway Act as being totally antiquated. "It's no doubt meant to be a bracelet and not a shackle," he says, "but there are times when I think our adornment is mid-Victorian in design, if not in purpose." He resents particularly the regulations that force him to continue the operation of obviously unprofitable lines.

This drain on C.N.R. revenues is small compared with the atonement it must make annually for its unnatural birth. The company was an unhappy amalgamation of four hundred railways, all virtually bankrupt, that couldn't be scrapped without isolating thousands of Canadians.

Following the success of the Canadian Pacific, promoters interested only in quick dollars built a wildly uneconomical conglomeration of railways. They over-capitalized them, squeezed out the profits, then pleaded bankruptcy. Because several Canadian banks and Canada's international credit position might have floundered with these shoddy roads, the Government reluctantly took over their operation. They were thrown together by Parliament in 1923, giving the C.N.R. a capital debt of well over $800 million at birth. Lord Atholstan, the *Montreal Star* publisher, seriously urged that the C.N.R. be assigned to the C.P.R. in exchange for a dollar bill.

During its first twenty-five years, the interest charges on

the C.N.R.'s dead weight of debt averaged $50 million a year, against an average net income available for the purpose of $30 million.

This debt load so limited operations that between 1931 and 1938, only seven new passenger coaches were acquired. The Toronto *Telegram* neatly summed up the feelings of many Canadians about some of the company's equipment. "The C.N.R. plans to mark the 100th anniversary of Ontario's first railway by creating a museum on wheels. It could save trouble by borrowing the Oakville–Toronto commuter train."

The transportation rush of war-time dramatically boosted the C.N.R.'s service requirements—the system carried 491 million tons of freight and 153 million passengers, including 6,735 troop trains. When Gordon arrived in 1950, he introduced a billion-dollar modernization scheme. This raised the C.N.R.'s assets to over three billion dollars, comprising lines into every province and into twelve states of the U.S.; hotels, ships, grain elevators, and other properties. Because the great bulk of company traffic produces little profit, Gordon estimates that one of his trains must haul a ton of freight two miles to buy him a new lead pencil.

When he compares the financial complexities of his railroad with the straightforward set-up of the Canadian Pacific Railway, Gordon sometimes ponders about the unintended irony of his mother in naming him after Donald A. Smith (Lord Strathcona), the fellow-Scot who was largely responsible for the C.P.R.'s original financing. Smith and Gordon were born forty miles apart in small milling towns in northwestern Scotland. Gordon was thirteen when his family left for Canada in 1914, the year Smith died.

Gordon's only railroading memory was the "Meldrum Maggie", an ancient wood-burner that shuffled the thirty miles between Oldmeldrum, his birthplace, and Aberdeen. His father was the village watchmaker, better known for the verses he wrote in local papers and the tales he told at the Masonic Temple about Jane, Duchess of Gordon, who in 1794 had enticed soldiers into the Gordon Highlanders by placing a guinea between her lips and allowing each recruit to kiss it away from her.

The Gordon business failed and the family emigrated to Canada, where young Donald at first helped pay the rent for their modest house on Claremont Street in Toronto by pulling out box ends at the plant of the Firstbrook Company. The six-dollar-a-week job ended when a truant officer forced him to attend Manning Avenue Public School. He acquired an after-class paper route, and invested ten dollars in a bicycle so that he could cover an area three times the usual territory. He enlisted the advantages of rail transport early in life by loading his papers on a street-car, then peddling furiously through the city to retrieve them at the end of the run.

His brief schooling terminated a year later, when he became junior clerk and deputy furnace man at the Bank of Nova Scotia's Ossington branch. He took every correspondence course available on banking, and impressed his manager so favourably that at twenty-three he was appointed to the bank's inspection staff—the youngest man ever to join that branch.

On one business trip to the Maritimes he missed his connection at St. Stephen, New Brunswick, but found some Toronto friends on the next train. With them was Maisie Barter, a dark-haired Newfoundland girl on her way to study at the University of Toronto. He talked to her all the way home and proposed six months later. The young couple enlivened the traditionally drab business of banking when one of Gordon's customers disappeared after a $1,500 loan granted on the collateral of a contract to write, produce and direct a series of radio dramas on station CKGW in Toronto. For thirteen weeks Gordon and his wife wrote one-act mystery plays, pressed neighbours into accepting parts, took the main roles themselves, and paid off the obligation.

The Gordons left Toronto for Ottawa in 1935 at the request of Graham Towers, the brilliant Royal Bank of Canada accountant chosen by R. B. Bennett to establish the country's central bank. Towers picked Gordon, who had by then become manager of the Bank of Nova Scotia Toronto branch, as his first secretary, and three years later promoted him to Deputy Governor of the Bank of Canada.

Donald Gordon's signature was printed on the lower left corner of Canadian banknotes, but the cloistered character of central banking kept him out of the news until exchange controls were imposed in 1939. In the fearful weeks before war was declared, the Canadian Government, through the Bank of Canada, mapped out rules to prevent dollars required for the war effort from slipping out of the country. On the day the announcement was to be made, Gordon summoned foreign-department officials of the chartered banks to Ottawa for briefing. He explained the new regulations to them in a locked conference room at the Bank of Canada, but would not allow them to inform their home offices. Other matters intervened and the order-in-council was not passed by the Cabinet until late in the evening. The bankers developed elaborate excuses to reach a telephone. One talked so much about a sudden illness that Gordon called in a stand-by nurse.

"And what," fussed one furious banker, "is going to happen to us if the Cabinet rejects the changes entirely?"

"Ah," Gordon replied with a great anticipatory grin, "then I shall have to shoot you all."

Gordon operated the foreign-exchange program with no sympathy for special situations. Canadian bankers were made to realize very quickly that he could be both reasonable and agreeable—provided he got his own way.

Meanwhile, another, far graver economic crisis was evolving in Canada's battle against inflation, due to the sudden demand for goods from a still immature industrial machine. Mackenzie King decided that a freeze would have to be clamped on prices. Impressed by Gordon's tough handling of the bankers, King appointed him to head the Wartime Prices & Trade Board, the organization set up for the difficult assignment. Gordon was only thirty-nine.

His first move was to call a national press conference in Ottawa. It was short and in character. "Some of you probably came here thinking that inflation is the only healthy answer," he began. "So we'll break off for ten minutes and give those who still feel that way a chance to leave the room." No one moved. "All right, then," he continued, "we'll go ahead on the assumption that everybody present accepts the basic credo of controls and ceilings.... Now you might just as well go home while I think this thing through. Down to *here*, I don't know anything about price ceilings, or how to make them work."

For the next five years Gordon led Canada's expedition into previously uncharted economic regions. His job was not only to flatten out prices, but also to allocate essential materials through civilian rationing. With cryptic haste he recruited the country's best business brains to help him. Typical was the wire he sent to Douglas Dewar, a leading Vancouver accountant : "DOUGLAS I NEED YOU." Dewar, puzzled but willing, replied : "WHERE AND WHEN?" Gordon shot back instantly : "HERE AND NOW." Dewar was in Ottawa working for Gordon forty-eight hours later.

Gordon enlisted the most respected man in each of the country's commercial and trade groups to become W.P.T.B. administrator. No industry could thus object—the orders came from a man who understood its problems, language, and techniques.

Lawyers on the Prices Board staff who drew up woolly-worded regulations were chastised with the comment : "Now I'm the corner grocer, and this doesn't make a damn bit of sense to me." When a file of gloomy undertakers crept into his office on Sparks Street to protest the Board's restrictions on cotton in casket linings, Gordon threw them out, and boomed after them : "If I die, the regulations will be relaxed !"

During a particularly touchy wage freeze, an angry Toronto convention of unionists challenged Gordon, who was visiting the city, to come and defend his rulings. The tension vanished instantly when he strode into the hall and announced : "Gentlemen, where I come from, a black-hearted bastard is a term of endearment."

His 1942 order banishing cuffs, patch pockets and vests from men's suits, prompted one reporter to ask : "I suppose, Mr. Gordon, that women's lingerie will be next."

"Yes," Gordon agreed, "our bodies may yet find themselves bulging for Canada, if they expect to depend on foundations."

Two months after Gordon's appointment, the cost-of-living index dropped sharply. During the entire war it rose only 20 per cent (mostly before 1941), compared with a 55 per cent jump in World War I. Gordon shared credit for the effectiveness of the price ceilings with Finance Minister James Ilsley, a Maritimer who rode to work on a street-car and ate most of his lunches at the hash counter of Bowles Restaurant.

At a 1947 banquet celebrating the dissolution of the Prices Board, Ilsley presented Gordon with a new Buick. "Donald Gordon," he said, "would never have succeeded had he sought to live up to the reputation of a dictator which his detractors gave him. He was forceful in expression and he did not mind a fight, but what the public got from Gordon was leadership, not dictation." Gordon thanked the minister for the car, ending his speech in typical style : "Sure I did a good job, and damn it, I'm proud of it."

As boss of the Wartime Prices & Trade Board, Gordon had done more to interfere with business than any Canadian before him, yet he returned to his Deputy Governorship at the Bank of Canada as one of the country's most respected administrators. "There will be some who will not agree with everything Donald Gordon did during his five years of absolute power over Canada's prices," editorialized *The Financial Post*, "but there will be few who will question his sincerity, his courage or his energy. Few if any could have handled such a gigantic and thankless task and left it perhaps the most popular man in Canada."

Saturday Night urged that Gordon should become a candidate for the federal prime ministership. In his farewell message to Gordon, Leon Henderson, the U.S. Price Controller, called him "the best damned price controller in the world".

No one was very much surprised that his post-war return to the Bank of Canada did not hold Gordon's interest long. Before he accepted the C.N.R. job he was offered the presidencies of two large Canadian banks and the chairmanship of the U.N.-affiliated International Bank for Reconstruction & Development.

"My current job is always the most interesting," he says. "The Wartime Prices & Trade Board was the most intensive position I ever held, the railroad has produced the biggest challenge, but I was happy at the Bank of Canada too."

Since his move to the C.N.R. Gordon has been approached to head the nationalized British railway system. One of the largest U.S. roads was anxious to alter its constitution requiring American citizenship of its presidents if he would become its chief executive. But Gordon has resisted all the offers. His explanation is simple. "Canada," he says, "is my kind of country."

chapter 11

E. P. T A Y L O R

*"Eddie can read a balance sheet like a poem,
and tell you where it doesn't scan."*

FLAG CAPTAIN Wilfrid Rupert Patterson, the commanding
officer of His Majesty's 35,000-ton battleship King George V
—two days out of Scapa Flow on her maiden voyage across
the submarine-infested North Atlantic—paced his bridge
pondering a minor but delicate problem of protocol.

According to fusty Royal Navy tradition, unchanged even
by the iconoclastic fury of the early 1940's, passengers aboard
ships of war were barred from officer's wardrooms unless
they paid a predetermined fee set by their rank in the mazy
hierachy of civilian life. This custom demanded that Lord

Halifax, on his way to Washington as the new British Ambassador, pay a toll of six guineas. C. D. Howe, director of Canada's armament program, returning home from talks in London, owed three guineas as a Minister of the Crown.

These were simple matters to settle. The Captain's problem was a blue-eyed, pink-jowled, tensely attractive but totally impatient passenger named Edward Plunket Taylor, who could not be fitted into any category provided by wardroom tradition. He had accompanied Howe to England for Canadian war-supply negotiations, and would soon be appointed by Winston Churchill as president of the British Supply Council, the United Kingdom's war-time purchasing agency in North America.

Captain Patterson glanced across the heaving grey sea at his destroyer escort, then made a snap decision: Taylor would, for this voyage, come under the guinea-a-day tariff extracted from the gaitered bishops of the Church of England.

Most Canadians would fatuously regard the good Captain's ruling as one of the war's cardinal blunders. But those who know E. P. Taylor and his methods more intimately insist it was the one perfect classification. No bishop ever believed his dogma with more compulsive dedication. Taylor's religion is business.

Taylor himself hotly denies this economic atheism. "I don't work at high pressure and I don't work for money," he insists. "Maybe I did initially, but certainly not now."

Such protests can be discounted by a fairly obvious fact: E. P. Taylor is the most successful Canadian businessman of his generation, and one of the most influential financiers in the world.

In mid-century Canada, Taylor has become as much a symbol as a man. He stands out in the classic struggle between the haves and the have-nots as the epitome of riches gained and business power wielded.

Canadians feel with a vague uneasiness that however they spend their pay cheques, they will inevitably enrich this grey-top-hatted eminence, pictured so often on the sports pages, binoculars perched on portly stomach, blandly accepting his latest racing trophy.

Taylor is condemned by socialists as "the crushing Croesus of big business", by Communists as "E(xcess) P(rofits) Taylor—the mad miser of millions", and by righteous temperance advocates as the beer baron personally responsible for the plight of every Canadian alcoholic. Even the established financial aristocracy regards with suspicion a colleague whose ferocious appetite for swallowing companies is unmatched in the annals of Canadian business.

Taylor is genuinely puzzled by these and other accusations. He insists that he is and always has been concerned with progress and achievement, not money and profit.

E. P. Taylor's personal creed is that of an unbridled entrepreneur who has mastered the workings of capitalism. He regards the free enterprise system primarily as a successful arrangement of human affairs in such a way that maximum benefits inevitably accrue to those who are the most adroit. He preaches that the good industrialist must do well for everyone—for his shareholders, customers and employees, as well as for himself. How, he asks, can you put an artificial limit on the size of business and still hope to preserve such a discipline?

Taylor's detractors maintain that he has mutilated the

free enterprise idea, which is meant to encourage venture capital into establishing new industry, thus raising the general standard of living. Of the hundred or so corporations within Taylor's orbit, he himself has established only three relatively insignificant firms. The balance of Taylor's industrial holdings are based on the acquisition of what others have built.

Using his grandfather's Brading Breweries Limited in Ottawa as the first link, Taylor has daisy-chained thirty breweries in Ontario, Quebec, Manitoba, Saskatchewan, Alberta, British Columbia and seven states of the U.S. into Canadian Breweries Limited. It is the world's largest brewing organization; sales average almost a million dollars a day. Taylor's other interests have made the group he heads a major influence in Canada's pulp and paper, chemical, agricultural implements, food, and merchandising industries. The unique financial maypole created by this enigmatic hustler has ribbons reaching into every corner of Canadian business.

Taylor's commonwealth of companies—cobwebbed through tiers of loosely connected holding subsidiaries—employs eighty thousand, has gross annual sales of $1½ billion, and indirectly affects the economic well-being of almost every Canadian family. The magnitude of this industrial complex is most dramatically illustrated by the fact that its sales account for a far greater proportion of Canada's gross national product than does General Motors in the context of the American economy. It is a curiously constructed empire, by no means integrated by either products or policy.

"I look for companies that will not only grow with the country, but faster than the country," Taylor says. "I look for companies where no very large shareholder exists. With my partners, I buy enough stock to give us effective control.

Then the company holds our view." In the process of expanding the flock of firms he shepherds, Taylor and his group have since the war channelled public investment of more than $600 million into new plant facilities.

Of the many misconceptions about Taylor, none is more prevalent than the belief that he *owns* all the firms with which he is associated. In Canadian Breweries, for instance, Taylor's personal ownership totals only 12,600 of the 3,069,411 issued shares, although Argus Corporation, the holding company he heads, carries on its books another 400,000 shares. In Argus itself, Taylor has about a quarter of the voting stock. This fraction plus the shares controlled by his partners give him 40 per cent of Argus' 1,370,272 shares. Argus, in turn, holds more than $117 million in stocks in Dominion Stores, Canadian Breweries, Massey-Ferguson, Dominion Tar & Chemical, St. Lawrence Corporation, and a few smaller firms. By being the largest single shareholder in each of these, with holdings ranging from $13\frac{3}{4}\%$ in Canadian Breweries to 22% in St. Lawrence Corporation, Argus can place enough directors on their boards to control policy.

All Argus companies bear one telltale mark: each includes the same four names in its board of directors—E. P. Taylor, W. Eric Phillips, M. Wallace McCutcheon, and John A. McDougald. Together, these men hold more than one hundred Canadian corporation directorships. "The Four Musketeers", a disgruntled competitor calls them.

Taylor has purposely made the idea of colonialism in running his empire as obsolete as it has become in politics. He refuses to concern himself with the administration of his companies beyond high matters of policy and finance—provided management continues to produce what he regards as a fair return on capital. "I like developing, not operating," he says. "I lose interest in a business situation when it begins to run smoothly."

When favour-seekers ask him to intercede with one of his firms, Taylor almost always tells them to see the president. "It's our policy," he says, "to find the right executives, to put them at the top, then to leave them alone to appoint their own employees right down the line."

Taylor invests only in companies whose policies he can guide. Because he won't buy speculative shares, Toronto stockbrokers have taken him off their mailing lists. He has thus deliberately cut himself off from any interest in the oil, gas and mining industries—the most buoyant sectors of Canada's post-war economy. "I make what capital I do," he says, "by buying cheaply, holding on, then expanding with efficient operations."

The diversity of Taylor's holdings is not accidental. "There are," he quips, "a few things hatching all the time." When he's asked how he can possibly manage to keep tabs on companies in such a wide variety of industries, he replies: "The answer is perfectly simple. I've got the knack of doing absolutely no administrative work whatsoever."

Taylor has an uncanny ability of thinking simultaneously along divergent lines. His mind works like a telephone exchange, switching from one set of company figures to another and back again without loss of continuity. "Eddie can read a balance sheet like a poem, and tell you where it doesn't scan," an associate once remarked admiringly. In his complex daily dealings Taylor seldom has to consult his files to recite the earned surplus, funded debt, depreciation, or profit of any of his companies—comparing the result by memory with previous years.

When he's at work behind his desk, Taylor's moods can be gauged by the interplay of his two favourite gestures; pointing an unlit Dunhill pipe or stroking his bulging chin with his left thumb. He likes to shave twice a day, enjoys all food except onions. He's a big man—six feet tall and two hundred pounds—and his cherry-cheerful face is grooved by pugnacity and laughter lines. Bushy brows overhang eyes of feral flint.

He is frank with most of his visitors to the point of ingenuousness, but maintains a layer of reserve few have breached. He is delighted when callers spread the impression of him as a tweedy squire more interested in horses than corporation finance. He begins telephone calls by chuckling: "This is Eddie."

Taylor's personal plans are formulated during the first week of each January. He dictates a memorandum to himself, outlining exactly what he intends to accomplish. It's also a good occasion for leafing through the resolutions of former years to compare visions with achievements.

Aside from his extensive horse-racing interests, Taylor has few diversions. He is not religious, but will occasionally attend St. John's Anglican Church, near his north Toronto home. Until recently, one of his great non-business interests was promotion of a world government system. "A parliament of the world," he declared in a speech shortly after World War II, "elected by the popular votes of democratic peoples, alone will save the world from chaos and anarchy. It's one world or none."

He once hired a Royal York dining-room to advance the

cause of world government, but cancelled his speech when only forty crackpots and professional joiners turned up. "You can't change people very quickly," he now admits. "I don't believe I could save the world."

The business passions of E. P. Taylor drive him a hundred thousand miles a year in constant commuting between his investments, partly aboard the private aircraft maintained by his companies. "After more than a week in one spot, I grow stale," he confesses. "I get my best ideas away from the office."

He has a house in Montreal, but has given up his permanent suite in New York's Carlton House, and maintains offices neither at Canadian Breweries nor at Argus. He spends most of his working time in the five-room cottage on his six-hundred-acre farm, off Toronto's Bayview Avenue that houses his personal staff of seven assistants.

The front of Taylor's office—furnished like a living-room with soft beige carpet and stone fireplace—is a picture window opening out on his estate. His desk is a simple oak table piled with documents. About the room are strewn *Racing Forms* and balance sheets. The library lining the north wall includes the *General Stud Book* and *Debrett's Peerage*, the guide to British nobility. Hunting scenes like *The Death of the Bear* and *The Hog at Bay* decorate the ante-rooms. Taylor usually arrives at nine in the morning, following a leisurely breakfast in bed, but his working day is erratic, often interrupted by visits to the track or his stables.

Despite his membership in nineteen clubs, Taylor's social contacts are deliberately limited. He attends few dinners and makes fewer speeches. His last great speaking tour was a thirty-nine-stop junket to raise funds for McGill University in 1948. He was for two years chairman of Toronto's Community Chest, and headed the Toronto General Hospital drive for $14 million, which collected $3 million more than its target. He has chaired the national fund-raising efforts for the Victorian Order of Nurses, as president of the Toronto Art Gallery has rearranged that institution's finances, and is one of the charter directors of the Canada Council.

One of his favourite social activities is to invite thirty or so of his friends to Sunday-night movies in the basement of his home. (He prefers Hollywood thrillers with happy endings.) The guests driving away from these soirées often speculate about the source of their host's remarkable business achievements. Someone inevitably remarks that, of course, it's not so difficult to become the country's richest man if you come from a rich family.

These are two of the many myths about Taylor. He did not inherit wealth, nor has he become the richest Canadian. Economists who have studied his holdings place his personal fortune at about thirty million dollars. That's far below the two men generally considered to be Canada's wealthiest— John David Eaton, who owns nearly all the stock in his family's retailing empire; and Samuel Bronfman, the head of Montreal's huge Distillers Corporation-Seagrams Limited, which through subsidiaries sells more than two million dollars' worth of liquor a day.

Taylor's father, Lt.-Col. Plunket Bourchier Taylor, was financially comfortable, but at his death in 1944 he left his son exactly $12,225 from an estate of $147,927. The elder Taylor, a sharpshooter in the Northwest Rebellion in 1885, had been second in command of Canada's 77th Battalion during World War I, and later managed the Bank Street branch of the Bank of Ottawa, founded and controlled by Charles Magee, his father-in-law. Another of Magee's investments was the local Brading Breweries, which survived the period of Ontario prohibition during the twenties by selling its products across the river to Hull, Que.

Young Eddie attended Ashbury College in Ottawa, then, following a summer interlude as a 25-cent-an-hour apprentice tool-grinder at the Ottawa Car Company, enrolled in McGill University's mechanical engineering course. Although he has since found his scientific training useful in appraising companies, when Taylor graduated in 1922, at the age of twenty-one, he began immediately to apply his promotional rather than technical talents.

His initial ventures were the Yellow Bus Company and Red Line Taxi, which he established with Lawrence Hart, now a Montreal business man. Hart and Taylor themselves drove trucks, which they had converted to buses, the five miles between Ottawa and Westboro. The bus line didn't last long; but the taxi firm, reorganized and profitably sold by the two ambitious youngsters, has since become Ottawa's largest.

Taylor then went to work for his father as partner in the Ottawa branch of the McLeod, Young, Weir & Company investment business. At the same time, his grandfather named him a director of his brewery. In 1927 he married Winifred Thornton Duguid, whose father had been in charge of Canada's shipbuilding program during World War I.

The grand strategy for the breweries merger that was the fountainhead of Taylor's corporate monarchy was nurtured, at least in part, out of boredom. Taylor (then concealing his youth with a moustache) moved to Toronto in 1927 and two years later became a full partner of McLeod, Young, Weir & Co. Prosperous and busy until the crash, he found that in 1930 few firms were interested in his underwriting services and even fewer clients wanted to buy into the market. Out of the Brading treasury, Taylor bought—for ten thousand dollars plus a million dollars' worth of Brading stock—the nearly bankrupt Kuntz brewery at Welland, Ont.

There were then in Ontario thirty-six breweries, competing for $17 million in annual sales with such wasteful vigour that only six companies were able to earn a minimum investment return. Beer was bottled in the province under 150 labels. The industry was working at 25 per cent capacity, slowly recovering from Ontario's 1916–1927 prohibition, when salesmen, distributing such business cards as *Bondy the Plasterer*, were paid 25 cents commission for each case they sold.

Taylor assembled all available financial facts about the Ontario breweries, then calculated how individual circumstances could be used to obtain their control. Instead of cash, he planned to trade pieces of paper for the properties by issuing shares in his newly formed Brewing Corporation of Ontario.

The scheme became operative when Taylor met Clark Jennison, an American promoter who had been given $750,000 by English financiers for investment in northern Ontario breweries. Taylor persuaded Jennison to back him instead. He brought Brading and Kuntz into the merger and on October 9, 1930, the Brewing Corporation of Ontario became the Brewing Corporation of Canada, assuming ownership of seven small plants. The name was changed to Canadian Breweries Limited on April 21, 1937. Jennison was named board chairman and Taylor, operating out of a cramped office in Toronto's Trust & Guaranty Building on Bay Street, was general manager.

He toiled sixteen hours a day, appropriating more and more plants, at the same time desperately trying to placate irate creditors who would neither understand nor back his bold manoeuvres. Taylor travelled around his growing platoon of breweries in a black Packard sedan fitted out as an office, cutting production costs and boosting sales. Within ten months Taylor reported to the company's seven thousand shareholders that he had gained control of ten breweries and a soft-drink firm. But his expansion pace was too rapid for the Brewing Corporation's still meagre financial resources. In the fall of 1931 he had to shift the pay-day at head office twice until enough sales receipts had accumulated to cover the payroll. When the foreman at the Dominion Brewery, a Toronto subsidiary, was told by his supplier that he could get a badly needed $25 length of rubber hose only by paying cash on delivery, the bill couldn't be paid. Although the brewing complex was running at only 16 per cent of capacity in 1931, four years later it showed its first profit of $168,000.

Jennison died of a heart attack while reading his morning paper at the Windsor Hotel in 1931, leaving the company's direction entirely to Taylor, who during the next two and a half decades acquired twenty-three rival breweries, eventually assembling an eleven-million-barrel brewing capacity. He liquidated a dozen of the more inefficient and reduced the brands from 150 to nine. His acquisitive tactics were "Taylored" to each situation. Some breweries, like the failing Riverside, Hofer, and Old Comrades, were brought in by buying into their mortgages, then foreclosing. Control in others, like the large Cosgrave plant, was gained by quiet stock purchases up to one-third control, followed by an offer to trade Brewing Corporation of Canada shares for the balance. The Carling Brewery in London, Ont., once owned by a Detroit company, was purchased in 1930 for $600,000 cash. O'Keefe's, the largest single acquisition, cost the Taylor syndicate $2,074,000, raised largely in England by floating more of the holding company's bonds.

When directors of the Canada Bud Company turned down Taylor's stock offers, he advertised his exchange deal directly to the shareholders. To sweeten the transaction, he helped raise the value of Brewing Corporation stock during the exchange period by instructing his London backers: "Put a substantial volume of orders into the market between June 11 and June 14 (1934) as this is a critical period . . . and the market quotation on our shares is of paramount importance to the success of the deal." The majority of Canada Bud holders turned in their stock; the company's directors capitulated.

The Federal Government's Restrictive Trade Practices Commission, which in 1955 investigated the formation of Canadian Breweries, found a confidential letter from Taylor to his English backers describing his early tactics. "We know," he wrote, referring to an enclosed list of ten small breweries, "that with consolidation an accomplished fact and half a million dollars cash in the bank, we would be in a position to make the operation of any one of the above listed companies so disastrous that they would be forced to consolidate with us or go out of business." In another letter, Taylor threatened "local price wars here and there to discipline small competitors." The Government study charged

Taylor with monopolistic attempts to dominate Canada's brewing industry. "Power," stated the report, "was obtained and competition was eliminated by deliberate, direct, intentional acts."

"Every move made in the building up of Canadian Breweries was reported to the shareholders. At no time were we told by any government that what was being done was wrong," Taylor shot back indignantly. The investigators did admit that Taylor's actions had not been able to prevent effective competition in the Canadian brewing industry and that he did not have the power to dictate prices.

During the quarter century following the formation of Taylor's brewing empire, his sales increased more than twentyfold, while Ontario beer consumption was only ten times as high. By 1952, Taylor's companies accounted for 71 per cent of Ontario's brewing capacity and fully one-half of Canadian beer sales. Canadian Breweries common stock moved from a low of twenty-five cents in 1931 to a high of $24 in 1949.

Canadian Breweries entered the U.S. beer market in 1933 by acquiring an interest in the Brewing Corporation of America, housed in the twenty-eight-acre Peerless Motor Car Company plant at Cleveland, which had been converted into a brewery following the 1933 repeal of Prohibition. By the end of World War II, Taylor owned 95 per cent of the company's stock. It seemed initially to be an investment lacking the Taylor touch—from 1946 to 1949 losses amounted to five million dollars and the firm ranked an insignificant sixty-seventh among American breweries.

Then Taylor placed George Black Jr., a Winnipeg chartered accountant he had met during the war, in charge, renamed the firm Carling Breweries Inc., and launched a major modernization and advertising program. Carling, within six years, moved into fifth spot among U.S. beer-makers—an unequalled growth record. While American brewing-industry sales increased at the rate of 2 per cent a year during that five-year interval, Carling's turn-over galloped ahead 32 per cent annually.

In Canada, meanwhile, Canadian Breweries continued multiplying its brood of plants. Post-war additions included three small Ontario units, the 1,200,000-barrel National Breweries Limited in Montreal (renamed Dow Brewery), Grant's Brewery in Winnipeg, and the huge Vancouver Breweries Limited, renamed Western Canada Breweries. The buying binge left Taylor with only four major Canadian competitors in the beer field.

Taylor planned and dominated every manoeuvre in the uninterrupted flourishing of his brewing complex, but during four critical years of its growth he was absent from all daily involvement. He left the company in 1940 to become Canada's second-youngest dollar-a-year man, first as a member of the Department of Munitions and Supply Executive Committee, later as executive assistant to C. D. Howe, the minister in charge.

Taylor and Howe went to England in the winter of 1940 to work out the Canadian industrial production schedules that would meet the United Kingdom's most urgent requirements. The careers of both these men—and it's difficult to pick two who have had more impact on the Canadian economy—very nearly ended about two hundred miles off the Irish coast at 6.05 A.M. on December 14, when a Nazi torpedo struck amidships the liner *Western Prince* in which they were travelling. The vessel sank so fast that Taylor didn't even have time to zip his pants on before leaping into one of the six lifeboats. The *Western Prince* survivors were picked up nine hours later by a tramp collier, but one man in Taylor's boat was dead from exposure and wounds. For a while, E. P. was nicknamed "Torpedo Taylor" by his friends.

When they returned to Ottawa, Howe sent Taylor to Washington as head of War Supplies Limited, the Crown agency charged with putting into effect the Roosevelt–King Hyde Park Agreement, designed to keep Canada off lend-lease. Under Taylor's direction, more than a billion dollars' worth of Canadian goods were sold in the U.S., helping to balance Canada's enormous trade deficit. Taylor's success in this difficult job came to the notice of Lord Beaverbrook, who recommended him to Winston Churchill as head of the new British Supply Council, formed to handle the more than fifty million dollars' worth of annual British buying in the U.S. and Canada. Taylor spent a week in daily conferences at 10 Downing Street with Winston Churchill, of whom he says : "He saved us. It's as simple as that."

It is now generally forgotten how many Canadians and Americans in high places defended Russia during World War II, not only as a valuable ally but even as a not unworthy political state. Taylor, incongruous as it now seems, was one of this group's most vocal members. "From my contact with the Russians," he told the 1942 annual meeting of the Canadian Manufacturers' Association, "I am convinced that the democratic world was guilty, before this war, of gravely misjudging our ally. While we cannot approve by any standard all of the methods used to create and maintain the U.S.S.R., I do feel that what motivated the Russian leaders and their people is of a much finer quality than we have been led to believe."

Taylor loved to repeat a story told him by Harry Hopkins, Roosevelt's emissary to Moscow, at a time when Stalin was still thought of as the benevolent if mysterious "Uncle Joe". On the night Hitler's invading army was battling for a city within a hundred miles of Moscow, according to this anecdote, Hopkins and Stalin sat chatting through an interpreter in the dictator's office. The only interruption was one phone call to Stalin. The translator leaned close to Hopkins, and whispered : "He is talking to his wife—he has been late for dinner three times this week and she's telling him that he positively must get home on time tonight."

Taylor's war efforts were recognized in July 1946, when he was made a Companion of St. Michael and St. George—the highest royal order that a Canadian civilian may accept. Fellow dollar-a-year men wondered why recognition had been given so late, but Ottawa pundits were certain that at least part of the reason was Taylor's war-time clash with Mackenzie King over the value of beer.

King in a 1941 radio address had urged Canadians to drink less beer because, he said, "too much alcohol adversely affects the efforts of the armed services and the munitions workers." Taylor snapped back with a press statement that described beer as a drink of moderation, a nourishing beverage. "A plentiful supply of it," he declared, "can make an important contribution to the well-being of the nation." In a private letter to King, Taylor warned the Prime Minister : "The professional prohibitionists are insatiable and will be back to you again and again, urging more and more restrictions which cannot help but create discord and disunity in our country."

The United Church of Canada demanded Taylor's resignation, claiming that his position as president of Canadian Breweries Limited was "a barrier to his loyal support of the Government and its policy of liquor restriction." Wesley United Church in Toronto distributed to its congregation a list of products made by Taylor companies, urging a boycott.

The protests did not interfere with the tempo of Taylor's war work. He was, by the winter of 1942, providing the most important personal co-ordinating link between the industrial war efforts of Canada, the United States and Great Britain.

Taylor spent three years in Washington working out of an office suite at the Willard Hotel. He kept in contact with the affairs of Canadian Breweries Limited through daily newsletters from vice-president Clive Betts and by flying to Toronto every second week-end. His working schedule was so tight that he dictated memoranda and letters in taxis to and from both airports.

Taylor resigned from World War II in the spring of 1944. "By then," he says, "I knew which side would win." He immediately ordered new brewing equipment for delivery the moment its makers switched to civilian production, thus placing his plants ahead of competitors in post-war modernization.

A month after his full-time return to civilian status, Taylor bought, for fifteen million dollars, the Victoria Lumber Company, one of the West Coast's largest timber firms. Within two years he negotiated four mergers with smaller mills to form the powerful B.C. Forest Products Limited, which has since become the third-largest producer of lumber in Canada. Argus now holds 11.6 per cent of B.C. Forest Products' stock, but control has been acquired by the Scott Paper Company, which owns 29 per cent.

Another early post-war venture was Taylor's entry into vegetable-oil production with his $2 million Victory Mills plant on the Toronto water-front. It was later sold to Procter & Gamble for $8 million.

During his first year in government service Taylor had lived in Ottawa's Chateau Laurier Hotel and dined often with James Duncan, another displaced industrialist, then serving as Deputy Minister for Air in the Department of National Defence. Duncan discussed with Taylor the great plans he had for the post-war expansion of Massey-Harris, the agricultural-implement firm he joined in 1911 and had risen to head. The company, founded in 1847 by Daniel Massey, who had supplied the farmers of Durham County in central Ontario with sap-boiling kettles, was even before World War II the Commonwealth's largest maker of farm machinery.

Taylor began to buy into Massey-Harris and in the winter of 1945, through Argus, acquired 55,000 of the company's preferred shares, transferring them into common stock one minute before the deadline specified by the company's by-laws—a move that wrenched control away from a syndicate headed by Toronto financier J. H. Gundy, a former partner of Sir Herbert Holt. With 8 per cent of the equity stock, Taylor became the largest single shareholder in Massey-Harris and immediately placed nine of his directors on the company's sixteen-man board.

Under Duncan's presidency, Massey-Harris sales increased fivefold between 1941 and 1955, but Taylor felt there had been too much emphasis on overseas operations. The 1952 average profit of 4.8 per cent had by 1955 dropped to 2.6 per cent. Despite record 1957 sales of $412 million, the year showed an over-all loss of $4.7 million. By May 1957 unsold inventory totalled $182 million.

Taylor, who by then had 30 per cent of the company's voting stock through his own and associated holdings, forced Duncan's resignation. "Duncan," he says, "is one of the world's greatest salesmen, but he surrounded himself with yes-men."

Duncan's dismissal, after forty-six years with the company, was publicly described as retirement due to ill health, although he took over the chairmanship of the Ontario Hydro-Electric Power Commission a few weeks later. At the time, Canadian businessmen who disapproved of Taylor pointed to the firing as litmus proof of his ruthlessness.

Taylor's reply was typical. "Me, ruthless? Certainly not. But when I'm right and management's consistently wrong, of course I get rid of management."

Eric Phillips, the most able industrialist in the Argus group, was chosen to ride herd over the company's reorganization. By October 31, 1958, Massey-Harris (renamed Massey-Ferguson) reported a jump from the previous year's loss of $4.7 million to a net profit of $13 million, with U.S. sales up 46 per cent. As part of the revamped merchandising campaign, an eight-girl chorus line went on a ten-thousand-mile corporate safari to enliven sales meetings.

The great concentrating instrument of Taylor's financial domain is Argus Corporation, named—not without purpose —after the son of Phrixus, the adventurer in Greek mythology who built the ship that discovered the Golden Fleece. Established in 1945 and modelled after New York financier Floyd Odlum's Atlas Corporation, Argus has introduced a new business medium to Canada.

Taylor describes his creation—a modified version of a closed-end investment fund—as "a special-situations company set up to acquire a sufficiently large percentage of control in carefully selected operating companies to effect an important voice in policy decisions."

In each of its extensions, Argus buys enough equity stock for effective control, but without tying up the excessive amounts of capital that would be needed to get absolute majority control. Another capital-stretching technique fully exploited by the Taylor group is capital borrowing. Argus started with equity capital of only $8.5 millions ($6 millions taken up by the directors) and preferred stock of $4 millions. As recently as 1957, Argus had notes and preferred stock outstanding equal to 44 per cent of its total net worth. "I have never," says Taylor, "been afraid to borrow."

Socialists and prohibitionists depict Argus as a carnivorous financial dragon—a picture incompatible with the tranquil, stenographer-lined corridors of the former Bank of Canada Toronto branch which the Taylor group bought in 1958 to house its administration. In order to instill an atmosphere befitting its rarefied dealings, Taylor had the Argus offices redecorated in mid-nineteenth-century style, with crystal chandeliers and Sheraton furniture. Argus has more directors (17) than officers (6) or employees (15). It annual report is a bland, folded-over single sheet of figures.

Despite Argus' innocuous physical trappings, there rests here a remarkable concentration of power. Its quiet mechanism guides a $117 million investment portfolio, so distributed that the company controls the destiny of industrial assets worth nearly a billion dollars in four of Canada's largest concerns—Canadian Breweries, Dominion Stores, Massey-Ferguson, and the St. Lawrence Corporation. Argus has experimented with other holdings—it once briefly controlled Peruvian International Airways—but expansion is now largely limited to fostering the growth of companies already held. The break-up value of Argus stock at its formation was $11. By 1959, despite several rights offerings, this value had climbed to more than $63. "If," claims Taylor, "we had put what capital we had in 1945 into bank stocks, we'd probably be better off today, and have none of the worries. But we deliberately set up Argus, because we think it's constructive."

One of the carefully fostered policies of Argus companies is to grant concessions to unions just a little ahead of their demands. "But," says Taylor, "we won't be pushed around." The method works. Canadian Breweries, for instance, has had only one brief strike.

Taylor's senior partners in Argus are Eric Phillips, who made his first fortune manufacturing glass in Oshawa; Wallace McCutcheon, a maths-and-physics graduate who was deputy chairman of Canada's Wartime Prices & Trade Board; and John A. McDougald, a graduate of Dominion Securities Limited.

A seldom revealed face of the Taylor business legend is the fact that some of his failures have been almost as spectacular as his successes. His ventures into publishing—*New World* magazine, through the Anglo-Canadian Publishing Company, and the *National Home Monthly,* through Stovel Press in Winnipeg—both flopped, although the latter was sold at a profit. His 1956 negotiations for the *Toronto Star* failed. He has since stayed away from publishing. When a reporter once asked him whether he was buying the Toronto *Telegram,* the city's other afternoon paper, Taylor cracked : "Sure, it costs me ten cents."

Probably Taylor's worst experience has been with Orange Crush and Canadian Food Products—both modelled on Canadian Breweries and designed to become dominant holding instruments in their industries. They flourished briefly after the war, but are now decidedly shoddy operations.

Taylor got into soft drinks involuntarily, through the acquisition of some ginger-ale subsidiaries along with his breweries. When in 1934 Orange Crush, which had been pioneered by a skating-rink concessionaire in west Toronto, was in financial trouble, Taylor paid $43,000 for stock once valued at $4.3 million. He eventually acquired eight bottling firms, but his soft-drink empire has since been barely able to stay in the black. It has been dropped from the Argus portfolio, although the Taylor group retains some equity.

Two days after Taylor's 1934 purchase into Orange Crush, he was notified of a lawsuit being brought against his new acquisition by Honey Dew Limited, in which Orange Crush had a small interest. To get the facts, he attended a Honey Dew board meeting and emerged as a vice-president, the court action postponed. A week later the Honey Dew president died. Taylor took over. He was now principal heir to the formula of Honey Dew's famous orange drink, and one of his initial jobs was to don a pair of overalls for mixing the weekly batch of concentrate. He eventually incorporated Honey Dew into a holding company he called Canadian

Food Products, and added three restaurant chains, a string of bakeries, and three chocolate plants. The restaurant division eventually became the largest chain of eateries in the country, operating 270 outlets. Annual sales of Canadian Food Products run around $20 million, but the profit margin has been so low that Taylor has removed the name from the Argus roster.

A relatively minor but increasingly successful member of the Argus family is Canadian Equity and Development, the holding arm for the Greater Hamilton Shopping Centre and Don Mills Development Limited, which in 1952 started building a $200 million satellite community to house 22,000 people and seventy industries on 2,200 acres eight miles north-east of downtown Toronto. It has since developed a similar project west of the city.

Taylor plunged more personally into real estate in 1956, after Harold Christie, a former associate of Sir Harry Oakes, approached him with the purchase offer for five thousand acres at Lyford Cay, fifteen miles west of Nassau, on New Providence Island. Taylor paid $2 million for the virgin scrubland, then spent $6 million improving it. He built an eighteen-hole championship golf course and a luxurious $2 million beach club. His one-and-a-half-acre beach lots sold for between $10,000 and $75,000.

He planned the resort as a retirement colony for English, Canadian and American businessmen, so that they might spend their last days sunning themselves in an atmosphere made tranquil by the realization that New Providence Island's administrators have not yet devised such refinements as personal income tax and death duty on real estate.

During his winter vacations at Lyford Cay, Taylor plays

golf (he's a powerful swinger but seldom breaks a hundred) and fishes off his own boat. It's equipped with a much-used radio-telephone capable of reaching Argus men in Toronto.

Taylor's main relaxation on the mainland is horse racing. He first became interested in breeding horses in 1935 when he set up a small racing stable with Jim Cosgrave. Mona Bell, one of his yearlings, placed second in the 1938 King's Plate—Canada's most highly regarded racing event. Taylor tried to win first place for the next eleven years, finally succeeding with Epic, in 1949. During the next decade, eight Taylor-bred horses captured the same honour—five under his own silks.

Taylor's $10 million farms at Oshawa and near Toronto have a hundred-man payroll and an $800,000 annual turnover. He makes no money on his equestrian subsidiaries but doesn't lose any either. As president and the largest shareowner (through Winfield Farms Limited) in the Jockey Club Limited, Taylor runs tracks that take in more than ninety million annual betting dollars. Almost half of Canada's racing is now run on tracks that Taylor controls.

The sales of the horses he breeds are designed to improve the quality of Canadian racing. There is no bidding. All the yearlings on his farms are catalogued with tags showing the records of their relatives and a suggested sales price. When half the animals have been sold, the balance remain under Taylor's colours.

His insistence that there is no point in winning, even in a horse race, against inferior competition, epitomizes Taylor's business philosophy.

The frenzies that move to action men of Taylor's calibre are always difficult to define. In Taylor's case it may simply be a matter of momentum—his inability to stop. "I get into so many things," he once complained, "because I just can't turn down situations which offer prospects of growth."

No final assessment of his impact on the country's economy can be made until Taylor's empire comes to be guided by other hands. But as Canadian business matures, the scope for the Taylor brand of genius will narrow, perhaps even vanish.

A free enterprise system that produced a dozen Taylors would, when these twelve men were pitted against one another, stiffen into an economic oligarchy. Taylor may well be remembered as the last of his type. Certainly he will be remembered.

EPILOGUE

With the punctilious flourish of a pope presuming worship, an unusual stranger stepped off the New York flight at Montreal's Dorval Airport on a squally spring afternoon in the late 1950's. He clamped a crown of galvanized iron askew on his wild shock of black hair, mounted a portable throne he had placed on the runway, and proclaimed himself King of Canada. "I have visited every country on God's earth," he announced. "And now I have come here to testify that this be the most blessed of all."

The self-styled monarch was Homer Tomlinson, general

overseer of a southern U.S. fundamentalist sect known as the Church of God. He flew back to more willing subjects in Tennessee two hours later, following a royal disagreement with Montreal immigration inspectors.

Homer's message was more pertinent than his dynasty. It has been endorsed—with less drama but more authority—by most of the free world's economists. In survey after survey, men who have spent their professional lives analyzing national development trends have chosen Canada as the land with the most buoyant business future.

This does not mean that through some fiscal miracle Canadians have been guaranteed eternal prosperity. Nor does it mean that we shall be spared the inelegant fumblings of the economically immature.

But there is *this* assurance to those who wonder whether opportunities still exist for careers on the scale described in the preceeding chapters: the simpler age that prompted into power men like Sir Herbert Holt, Lord Strathcona, Sir William Van Horne, Sir Harry Oakes, and Sir James Dunn is forever gone, but the chances for different, and in many ways more enduring business greatness have never been better.

Although Canada is politically less than a century old and our population is little more than twice that of New York City, the acquisitive itch of the men in this book and legions of their contemporaries has made this country the sixth-largest industrial and fourth-greatest trading nation on earth.

Those who regard this remarkable achievement as having made further economic pioneering obsolete should remember that at least two-thirds of Canada's resources remain un-mapped, even on a reconnaisance scale, and that despite our attainment of the world's second-highest living standard, about a quarter of our homes still lack even the basic convenience of a bathtub. In some of the fundamentals of advanced civilization, our neglect has been formidable : the Canadian economy could run full-out for half a decade merely filling the gaps in our school, highway, hospital, water and sewerage requirements.

No country places as few geographical limitations on dreams of business empire as Canada. Seven time zones are required to accommodate the outrageous dimensions of the Canadian sub-continent. When it's a dusky 5.30 P.M. in Newfoundland, church bells toll high noon across the Yukon.

Canada covers one-fourteenth of the earth's surface, but less than 7 per cent of her land has been exploited, or even occupied. Nine out of ten Canadians live in a Chile-like strip along the American border—and even here, only an average of twelve people inhabit each square mile. Most of Canada's hinterland abides silent, unexplored and inaccessible. A drive three hundred miles north from any Canadian city ends in primeval wilderness.

The men in this book were preoccupied with extending Canadian economic development beyond the barren granite inlay of the Canadian Shield. Many of tomorrow's Canadian business princes will build their domains under the wide sub-Arctic horizon, where birch trees take a century to grow twelve inches and indigo delphiniums sprout six feet in one nightless summer.

Before the stirrings of their ambition turned the thoughts of this book's entrepreneurs westward, the Prairies were generally regarded as uninhabitable wilderness. The inheritors of financial grandeur in Canada will be the men who first realize, on a sufficiently magnificent scale, that our north can shed a similar stigma, in a taming like that already achieved by Russia. There five million people live and work permanently in regions climatically comparable to territory in Canada that is now occupied by a scattering of thirty thousand pioneers.

Canadians have already begun hesitantly to poke about the uncounted hillocks of riches undulating across the halcyon desolation of the north. For some, fortune impatiently attends their decision to seek beneath the crunch of their footsteps. The land gently whispering to us beyond the insulation of big-city comforts has been described by George Weaver, the former M.P. from Churchill, Manitoba, as "a treasure house beside which the fabulous wealth accessible to the genie of Aladdin's Lamp was peanuts."

Preliminary drilling suggests that the inhospitable Devonian limestone of the Mackenzie River Delta may cloak an oil potential greater than that of Alberta. The lathery pools puncturing Ellesmere Island, six hundred miles inside the Arctic Circle, may hold more oil than Saudi Arabia. In the tar sands of Athabaska are locked from one to three times the world's proven oil reserves. Out of the frowning cliffs that drop into Hudson Bay from the Belcher Islands will come iron ore in billions of tons. The world's largest lead-zinc deposit stretches, a hundred feet thick, for thirty-six miles along the solitary shore of Great Slave Lake. The mightiest untouched hydro potential on earth—an ultimate five million horsepower—roars to waste at Grand Falls, on the Hamilton River, foaming its way down seventeen hundred feet from the upper Labrador plateau into Lake Melville.

The subjugation of northern resources represents only one

potential source of future Canadian fortunes. Immense personal rewards will be gained by those who master the organizational, financial, and technical skills involved in the accelerating transition of the Canadian economy from its agricultural roots to mature industrialization. Twenty years ago, one-third of working Canadians toiled on farms; if present estimates are correct, twenty years from now only one-seventh of the labour force will be farming. The balance of the nation's efforts will be increasingly expended in secondary manufacturing and construction.

Tomorrow's Holts, Dunns and Taylors will not only be the men who forecast most ably our industrial needs, but also those who capitalize most skilfully on the resultant gush of living-space requirements. Our cities will cascade over their boundaries, smothering villages and their orchards. To stab new apartment towers at the sky and to set down on the Canadian landscape enough new satellite communities to accommodate the coming urban multiplication, will require the scooping out of excavations equivalent to two St. Lawrence Seaways by 1985.

The expected doubling of our population within the next three decades will spawn new Canadian merchandising dynasties. With our birth rate one of the highest of any industrialized nation, Canadian business is currently gaining forty-six new customers (including immigrants) per hour. That's enough, in a day, to support an extra grocery store, enough in a week for a new supermarket.

Accompanying our postwar population growth and the resultant burgeoning of business opportunities has come an unprecedented influx of American and other capital, which has given Canada more foreign investment within its borders than any other country in the world. The deluge of U.S. investment funds—gushing across the border at the fantastic gross rate of almost three million dollars a day since 1945—has engulfed our profit-making enterprises to an extent that has reduced Canadians to holding squatters' rights in many industrial categories. American businessmen have appropriated more than three-quarters of our petroleum production, half of our manufacturing, mining and forest industries.

The Americans have not come here in the tradition of the sixteenth-century conquistadores. In the process of their profit-ferreting, they have underwritten the development risks, reducing from generations to years the time required for Canadians to attain their current standard of living. But if this country hopes to retain long-term control of its economic destiny, Canadian businessmen must recapture at least part of these industrial and mineral assets, reverting the profits they yield to domestic command.

Other future barons of Canadian wealth will derive their dollars from the coming shift in working-hour patterns. A hundred years ago, man strained for a little time to see the sun without having to squint at it through factory and office windows. The ensuing struggle for shorter working hours has been so spectacularly successful that the thirty-hour week will as surely result from automation's taking over an increasing number of production processes as the forty-hour week was the outgrowth of assembly-line techniques. The week-end, set at one day by the Fourth Commandment, will, for at least some of the twelve million Canadians now under forty, become a weekly three-day vacation.

This extra leisure could usher in an exciting new kind of existence, with the worries of work no longer dominant in the emotional landscape. Or the abundance of free time could bring the burden of a fallow living pattern, with most Canadians collapsed in front of their television sets, doctoring new martini mixes.

The leisure we already have poses in a major way the problem of how to escape boredom. Canadians own the highest per capita ratio of pleasure boats in the world; twice as many students as are enrolled in our universities prance about at dancing schools. Canadians now spend more than three billion dollars a year—the equivalent of two basic steel industries—satisfying their leisure-time desires. These expenditures will double by 1975.

Future sources of Canada's entrepreneurial fortunes have been shown to exist in exploitation of the north, extension of secondary manufacturing, participation in the explosive growth of urban housing, formation of merchandising outlets to feed and equip the burgeoning population, reappropriation of Canadian assets now controlled by Americans, and gratification of multiplying leisure's new demands. Men who lack the unhampered dash to create their own financial empires in these categories will have to find the genesis of their business power in managing the economic inspiration of others.

The classic entrepreneur treated his managers like hired hands. But as corporate ownership has swung from slam-bang individualists to security-conscious shareholders, the guidance of business enterprise has increasingly become the burden of professional executives, a breed not older than the modern corporation.

Youngsters without special privileges or aptitudes once could hope to move at least into the elementary tiers of the management group simply by following the Horatio Alger criteria of toiling from sunup to sundown, eschewing even the most venial vices and speaking respectfully to the boss and all his relatives. Acolytes in tomorrow's temples of business will be faced with a changed and increasingly complex set of rules. The wrench beyond the elementary rungs of responsibility will take metal in the soul.

The competent and ruthless will manipulate themselves upward much more quickly than rivals who are only competent. Successful managers will be as cold and calculating in planning their careers as corporations have become in setting sales targets. They will have to identify themselves with their economic ambitions so thoroughly that they'll accept corporate actions and philosophies as genuine extensions of their personal feelings.

Such iron-hearted loyalty will not extend to the successful executive's superiors. Disagreement with presidential decisions will be expressed in deliberate authority-destroying rebellion. Some of these restless aggressors will be fired; others will become—until they in turn are deposed—the most imaginative managers this country has ever had.

It will increasingly be good judgement, not formal knowledge, that will launch men toward executive status. Those who come up too constantly with quick answers to their superiors' queries, will disqualify themselves for business leadership. The hunt is on for visionaries—fast answers are based, almost always, on what has happened in the past, not on what might be.

The executive tugging for success in the super-competitive environment of the evolving Canadian corporation will have to sit perpetually on the edge of his chair—prepared, when his clairvoyance fails, to be buried where he falls. He will have to pay in full measure for every new foothold on his upward climb, in terms of loss of privacy, the inability to plan according to personal feeling, and loneliness. Decisions formerly taken following friendly consultation with equals will have to be made in the personal isolation of a Holt struggling to contain his beleaguered business empire.

As in the other arts, the results of successful management are obvious, its means mysterious. This book demonstrates that no basic behaviour pattern exists which, if followed, will take a businessman to the top.

What changes a man into an executive is not his move behind a polished mahogany desk. It is a gradual shift in his attitude toward work—a magic transformation that occurred to the men in this book at the point when their hearts and brains lost the energy to stay out of constant economic embroilment.

Their flame of power, fanned by this inner frenzy, burned so brightly because they maintained one common faith: they believed that, under free enterprise, man loses his opportunity for business greatness only when he abandons his quest.

ACKNOWLEDGEMENTS

FOR his patient guidance of, I am sure, an often exasperating pupil in the writing art, I am particularly thankful to Ian Sclanders, the articles editor of *Maclean's Magazine*. I wish as well to acknowledge the imaginative leadership of Ralph Allen, editor of *Maclean's*, and to thank him for permission to use, as part of my research for Chapters VI and IX, material I originally gathered for his magazine.

For her initial support I am grateful to Patricia Newman. Much of this book really belongs to her. I am also under heavy obligation to R. A. Browne of Longmans, the publisher who conceived this volume; C. C. "Chuck" Milne, news editor of *The Financial Post*, who taught me so much; Harry Chapin Plummer, my old and wise Montreal friend; Mrs. Jean B. Mackay and Mrs. Barbara Maguire, the ever-helpful librarians of the Maclean-Hunter Publishing Company; and Martin Lynch, a bearded genius whose friendship encouraged me, while his knowledge aided and amazed me. My greatest debt is to Christina McCall, for her creative editing and inspiration.

This book owes its existence to the aid and encouragement of many others not mentioned here; only the responsibility for imperfections is fully my own.

Peter C. Newman.

PORT CREDIT, 1956—OTTAWA, 1959.

INDEX

INDEX 263